BELFAST STORIES

SAM McAUGHTRY

THE
BLACKSTAFF
PRESS

BELFAST

First published in 1981 by
Ward River Press Limited

This Blackstaff Press edition is a photolithographic facsimile
of the 1981 edition printed by Cahill Printers Limited,
East Wall Road, Dublin 3

This edition published in 1993 by
The Blackstaff Press Limited
3 Galway Park, Dundonald, Belfast BT16 0AN, Northern Ireland

Printed in England by
Cox and Wyman Limited

A catalogue record for this book
is available from the British Library

ISBN 0-85640-520-5

Contents

Belfast and Beyond

The Man With No Nerves

I took a mouthful out of my first pint. It tasted a bit tacky. 'Do you not think that pint's on the tacky side?' I asked old Johnny Robinson, sitting beside me. 'It's terrible, that's what it is,' he said, screwing his face up, 'it's just as bad a pint as I have had to suffer this long and many's a day.'

His own glass was half full. He sat studying it for a minute, in the light of what we'd been saying, then he picked it up and knocked it back in what can only be described as a blur of movement. He shuddered. 'Rotten,' he said: then he shouted for attention: 'Give us another pint,' he yelled, 'and this time it's porter I want, not bitter aloes.'

Harry the barman, who thought he looked a bit like John Travolta, tore himself away from the mirror, and pulled another drink. When the fresh pint was put in front of old Johnny he caught it before it touched the table and hoovered the half of it down him in an instant. Then he sat back with a faraway look on his face, smacking his tongue and licking his lips. He lifted the glass and studied its contents: 'That pint's desperate,' he shouted to the barman, 'it's a wonder you've the nerve to offer it for sale.' Then, in the same time that it would have taken me to push a strand of hair off my brow he had the pint down him, and out of the road. He loosened the bottom button of his waistcoat, and sat back.

I made up my mind to switch drinks: the pint was like varnish. 'Give me a rum and pep,' I said. I turned to old Johnny: 'Will you take one?' I asked him. 'I will, thank you,' he said at once, 'I'll take another pint.'

Up at the bar, I said to Harry: 'How can he complain about it, and still keep on knocking it back?' 'I never even try to work that sort of problem out,' Harry said, 'my job's to keep the customers supplied with lunatic broth. If I ever tried to get into the minds of these space cadets I would end up getting electric shock therapy.' He served up the drinks and went back to studying his profile in the mirror.

'There's no doubt about it,' old Johnny said, when I put the drink in front of him, 'there's no pints could stand up to the ones long ago. Six pints of Double in the 1930's, and you were liable to jap your brains out against a lamp post on the way home, that's what I call gravity. Here's the best respects,' and he lowered the whole pint in one go. It was out of the way before I had time to raise my own glass.

I sat studying him. He was a big man, well-built, and very contented. His red and purple nose was testimony to a life's work, studying porter in all its moods. 'You're no mug at massacring the pints,' I said, 'you despatched that one so fast that the glass is actually palpitating.'

Old Johnny snorted. 'You should have seen me when I was a young man,' he said, 'I was a tram driver, you know. When I reached the terminus at Glengormley I could have stepped off the tram, into the pub at the road ends, put two pints down me, and been back ready to drive the tram before the conductor had the trolley turned around.' He looked at me sideways: 'Do you want to see me when I'm in a hurry?' he asked. I gave Harry the nod, telling myself philosophically that all learning has to be paid for, one way or the other. Harry bent to his task. 'By the way,' old Johnny called to him, 'there was a definite vinegary taste off that last one. It's gradually coming back to normal.'

'Now before that pint goes the road of all the other ones,' I said, 'could you explain to me exactly why it is that you can sink them so fast?' 'I'll do better than that,' he said, 'I'll demonstrate it for you.' He lifted his glass, 'but mind you,' he said severely, 'I can never properly enjoy demonstration pints.' I nodded resignedly: it was only money.

He opened his mouth, tilted the glass, and slowly let the drink run down. There wasn't even the trace of a tremor about the muscles of his throat. It was as if they were made of marble. 'That's amazing,' I said, 'it's just as though you were putting it into a jug.'

'It's the nerves in my throat,' he said, 'they're dead.'

'Was it rushing the pints when you were a tram driver?' I asked him. 'No,' says he, 'it must have happened in my first job. I was a barman for years', he explained. While Harry drew the next one he went into detail. 'This old publican I worked for was proper tight,' he said, 'he wouldn't have given you a thick penny for a thin one. And he never left the barmen alone in the bar. He watched us like a hawk, hardly turning his back on us. When I was drawing pints at the barrels I used to wait till he turned towards the till, then I would have drunk maybe an inch or so. Gradually I increased the amount, until eventually I was able to drink a pint in less time than it takes most people to order one.'

'A similar story to Hackenschmidt,' I said, 'he began learning his strong man act by lifting a calf. And he lifted it every morning. So eventually he was able to lift a fully grown cow.'

Old Johnny Robinson took hold of the last pint he was going to get from me that night: he looked at it critically: 'It's still not a great pint that,' he said. He gave himself a twitch, to loosen himself up, like a gunfighter about to draw. Then, so fast that the movement was broken up into separate images under the alternating current of the electric light, he sank the pint in what must have been the merest fraction of a second. 'I wish it was closing time, till I get away home out of this,' he said, 'them pints is holy murder.'

The TV Scoop

About twenty years ago, when the English were about to make gambling legal, the BBC sent their famous TV interviewer Colin Flicker over to Belfast to report on the betting scene for television. Roughly — very roughly — here's how it went.

He ended up in a bookie's pitch down near Donegall Street, and proceeded to set up his interview. 'Tell me,' he said to a big man of about twenty-five from the Shankill Road direction, 'do you come here to the betting shop often?'

'I'm never out of it,' said your man.

'I see', the TV reporter nodded seriously, well pleased with the way things were kicking off, 'and do you bet much?'

'Every chance I get,' his subject replied.

Colin Flicker was all delighted with himself: 'And how much would you put on for a wager?' he asked. 'It would depend on how much I had,' the other said, 'I would put whatever I had on.'

'My goodness!' The interviewer was visibly surprised. He looked at the camera to see whether it was surprised as well. It was every bit as amazed as he was. 'Where do you get the money?' he wanted to know.

'From anybody who'll give it to me,' the big lad told him, 'I would even try asking my old mother for it, if I thought she'd any left'.

Colin Flicker turned and looked full into the

camera significantly. He gave the viewing millions a decent period to get over their shock. Meanwhile your man, smiling politely was patiently waiting for the next question. It came: and it was a good one, too.

'Are you working, by the way?' the famous man asked, with elaborate casualness. 'Not at all,' his subject said, 'oh, not at all. Not a bit o' me's working. Oh no.'

Colin Flicker's mouth fell open. 'Unemployed!' he gasped, 'yet you borrow money to bet?' He shook his head, speechless. He turned to see whether the camera was still with him: it was. It was staring straight at the big Shankill Road man as he stood there, completely at ease, smiling at the bet-starved millions on the mainland.

The interviewer had recovered enough to put another, penetrating, question. 'Tell me' he asked, eyeball to eyeball with his interviewee, 'have you ever actually been to a race meeting?'

'D'ye mean like Leopardstown?' the big fellow asked. Colin Flicker nodded. 'I mean an actual race track,' he said, 'have you ever been to one? Have you seen a horse race, in fact?'

'Oh no', your man said, 'not at all. Oh no. Damn the race ever I would go to.'

It was the perfect note to finish on. Turning to the camera after a pregnant pause, the TV star said: 'This is Colin Flicker. I return you now to the studio, from Belfast, where the betting shop is an established way of life'.

And in the studio that evening Cliff Michelmore smiled, shook his head in disbelief, and said: 'The Betting and Gaming Act reaches the statute book in a few days' time'. Then he moved to the next business, and the great British public poured itself a second cup of tea, and pondered on the nature of the revolution that was soon to hit them, when the betting shops opened in the High Streets of Middle Wallop, and Waggling Parva.

Back in the bookies in Belfast the sound equipment and the lighting were packed up and the interviewer thanked his subject most politely. Then the TV men headed for the Brown Horse for a snifter, well pleased with themselves.

All around, within the bookies, business had never stopped. In fact the punters had hardly noticed the interview taking place. During the whole rigmarole they had continued to study the Sporting Chronicle, place their bets, pray in silence, curse not just so silently, and hurl torn-up dockets to the ground. Interviews could come and interviews could go: it was all one to the punters. Colin Flicker could have been questioning the Wandering Jew, asking him what brought him to this side of the Irish Sea, for all the punters cared. It takes a very great deal to break into the concentration of a Belfast betting man.

Next day, in the pub next door to the bookies, I met the big man from the Shankill Road. 'You're getting worse,' I told him, 'what were you doing in the bookies anyway?'

'Ach, I was looking for our Andy', he said. He laughed: 'You know our Andy: horses on the brain. What he sees in them I don't know. . . . . .'

Unlucky Jim

In all my life I've never met anybody with such peculiar luck as our Jim. I'll give you an example: one night about twenty years ago he came into possession of information about a brindle dog running in the third race at Dunmore Park. He was carrying a fiver for it; I went along to watch.

The two of us spectated at the first race. First races at the dogs are only for spectating: form's just a hollow joke with the dogs that are taking part. But when the second race came up our Jim thought the favourite was pitched in: 'It'll be going so fast up the home straight that it's liable to burst through the fence and right on to the Antrim Road,' he said. It was possible to get even money about it if your eyesight was good, and our Jim had many-sided vision like a fly. He found a bookie who was laying evens and against my advice he had the fiver on it.

Well, his confidence proved to be soundly based. The dog came out like a rat going up a spout. It went so far ahead that the other dogs must have thought it was the electric hare. Down our Jim went and collected his tenner.

'Right,' he said, when the bookies started to lay the third race, 'now for some folding money.' He took the two fivers out, fanned them open in his hand, held them up in front of him, and bounded down the steps of the stand to try for the best odds he could get. 'Twenty five pound to ten,' he shouted to one bookie, holding the money up. The bookie gave him an old-fashioned look: 'You're a fiver short,' he said. Our Jim looked at the money still clutched in his hand; sure enough, one of the fivers was missing. As he'd run down the stand some quick-witted punter with lightning reflexes had said thank you very much and twitched one of the notes out of his hand.

So it was as if he'd never risked his stake in the previous race: it had all been for nothing. Our Jim was so upset that he went off the tip and backed one at a bigger price to try and make up for the loss. Needless to say, the tip won easily.

That's our Jim, a man with a strange and baffling mixture of good and bad luck.

He was sent out by his wife to buy some paint one Saturday, and he happened on me in Dempsey's bar. 'Have you time for one?' I asked him. 'Only the one let it be,' he said, 'I'm out for paint on the wife's orders and with her money, for I've none of my own.' 'You don't need to tell me that,' I said, 'no man worth the name would paint the house on a Saturday while he had betting money in his pocket.'

As I was talking our Jim had been running his eye over the paper: 'Is that Duke of York I see in a two-mile race at Ascot?' he asked. 'The very same,' says I. He takes another look, then he gave a jump: 'Black Prince,' he said, 'in the sprint. What a coincidence.' I looked blank. 'These royal names,' he said, 'and they're running at Royal Ascot. And another thing,' he went on, 'what sort of paint was I sent out to get?' 'Black paint?' I suggested, trying to get a connection with the Black Prince, but he shook his head in disgust. 'Black paint?'

he repeated, 'do you think I live in a toolshed or something?' 'Well, I was only trying to humour you,' I said. 'I was sent out,' says our Jim, slowly and deliberately, 'to buy Crown paint: do you get it now?' And with that in he goes and shoves the paint money on to a double, Duke of York and Black Prince.

He got Duke of York up but Black Prince was pipped on the post. I started to sympathise with him, but he stopped me: 'Did you not see who owned the horse that beat me?' he asked. I shook my head. 'It was owned by the Queen Mother,' he said, sadly, 'the indications were there: it was only a matter of looking for them,' and away home he went paintless.

But his worst experience happened when he got the tip for the Ballymena dog. Eddie Turner, confidant of trainers, promised to release the name of the dog to our Jim only after Eddie himself had backed it at the track that night. This was a familiar security precaution. Our Jim promised faithfully to tell nobody about it, but he actually told one man, and that man was Bobby McArdle, who was related to the starter. Bobby swore on the Bible, the Koran and the Sporting Chronicle to tell nobody else.

Up they went to Dunmore Park, with our Jim sticking to Eddie Turner and Bobby McArdle sticking to our Jim, and a whole army sticking to Bobby McArdle that our poor Jim knew nothing about.

A couple of minutes before the off Eddie Turner slipped over to the bookie and backed the dog. This is the critical time, for bookies are hypersensitive to moves of this sort. They have built-in seismographs that register the slightest tremor in their market. It was vital for our Jim's plans that he should slide just as quietly to another bookie and get his few quid on, immediately afterwards, but what does he do but tell Bobby McArdle the name of the dog first, before he makes his move. And as soon as your man Bobby learns the tip he immediately turns to his legion of followers and holds up fingers to show the dog's number.

Well, you talk about a dive. The bookies were nearly carried off their stands. Our Jim couldn't get near them to make his own bet. By the time the crowds thinned the race was off and it was too late. He had to stand there and watch the tip racing home alone. And worse than that, he had to watch Bobby McArdle collecting his commissions from the punters he had tipped off. The final straw came when Eddie Turner blew him out. 'That's the last turn I'll do you,' Eddie said, 'you're worse than Reuter's for spreading news.'

To tell you the truth, after that our Jim went out to Australia. I can't say I blame him. If it had been me, I'd have gone off to the Antarctic. There's no racing there at all.

The Man Who Didn't Know

There was a wee cockney man used to get into Dempsey's bar a lot of years ago, and if ever a man was dying to make friends he was. He was chirpy, and cheerful, and if he ever got into company he wasn't behind the door in standing his round. On top of that this fellow had a good stock of jokes, so he could keep his end up in the line of conversation and that.

Now for some reason Belfast people nearly all treat men with English accents with the best of respect. It's assumed that they're all highly educated, I suppose, or what's more likely, it's assumed that the English couldn't possibly be less educated than the Belfast people. Yet that wasn't the case with this wee cockney. The respect wasn't there.

Nobody was exactly rude to him, mind you. Very far from it. When he mentioned current affairs, or football, or the weather or that, the people near him at the bar would have nodded politely, or murmured something non-committal. But he could never get right into the life of Dempsey's. He wasn't a part of the place.

And yet you could see he liked our company. Even when he was standing at the counter on his own, and somebody made a bit of a joke, the cockney would laugh quietly to himself, maybe looking sideways, to see if his laughing would open the way to an invite into some company or other. But it didn't.

Sooner or later he was bound to bring the matter up with me, for his time for an after-work pint used to coincide with mine, and we would find ourselves together at the bar a fair amount, because in those days my idea of an after-work pint was actually about four pints, and that takes time. About twenty minutes.

I was embarrassed when he introduced the sub-ject: 'Why don't they like me here?' he asked. I began to bluff it out a bit, at first. 'Maybe you're only imagining it,' I said, but he was insistent. I thought it over carefully for a minute or so, then I shrugged: it would only be doing the man a kind-ness to tell him. Obviously he would have to know some time, and the experience could easily prove a painful one for him, if one or two other customers I could think of ever took it into their heads to put him right.

'It's actually to do with the horses,' I began. He looked astonished: 'The 'osses?' he repeated. I nodded my head. I think he was relieved. He pro-bably expected me to open up with Oliver Crom-well.

After the initial awkwardness the words came more easily to me. I started to explain the back-ground to him.

'You might think,' says I, 'that backing a horse is only a cash transaction, but it's a very great deal more. .' And I outlined to him the vital importance of keeping to the protocol during racing hours. He listened intently.

A five furlong sprint takes a couple of minutes. So when the bet's put on, you would think the whole thing would be over and done with when the result comes in, wouldn't you? Well, you would if you were a cockney, I suppose. But that's not always the case in Belfast.

You've done your bet, right? Well, the next thing you do is to get out of the bookies and up to the bar counter. From then on you don't make mention of racing, or odds, or anything pertaining to the gamble. You talk to your companions about natural science, or astronomy, or veterinary medicine, or anything, to take your mind off the bet. You see by the clock that the race is on; then you see by the same clock that it's over. Punters come into the bar from the bookies, and you know perfectly well that they know the result. But you don't ask, and they don't tell. They never tell.

Right, you give yourself a good ten minutes, then you walk into the bookies. But you don't look up at the board for the result right away. Oh no. What you do is you go over to one of the newspapers, keeping your eyes averted from the board. You also close off your ears from the noise around you, in case you might accidentally hear the result. You do this by exerting nervous pressure on your eustachian tubes, thus causing a mighty rushing sound to fill your head, and this drowns out the external noises.

You stare at some inconsequential thing or other in the newspaper, maybe an advert: 'At Stud,' it might say, 'Chestnut by Sunstroke, out of a mare by Loppylugs. No foal no fee.' You pretend to be interested in this: 'Imagine that,' you say to yourself, 'no foal no fee.' But your eyes are moving slowly upwards, five degrees at a time, to the result board.

And here's where the bookie helps you, with your ritual. He knows about it, you see, so he has employed a man to mark the results up who can hardly write. When your eyes actually reach the board your final, delicious, effort, is to decipher the hieroglyphics that pass in a Belfast bookie's office for characters of the English language. Then, and finally, you admit the result of the race to your conscious mind.

'That,' says I to the cockney, 'is something that doesn't need explaining to the native Irish. But,' and here I looked at him severely, 'it doesn't half need explaining to you.' I fell silent. My work, unpleasant though it had been, was finished. I felt the better for it.

A new light was dawning in the cockney's eyes. 'Gorblimey,' he said, 'what a bleeding fool I've been.'

I nodded. 'Yes,' I said. 'You walk in through that door, stand just inside it, and shout, without giving one of us a chance to make the rushing noise: "The favourite's beaten!" you shout. It's a wonder you haven't been run out of town on a rail.'

The cockney was nearly in tears. 'Will they ever forgive me?' he asked. Slowly I shook my head.

Forlornly, he walked through the door, and he has never been seen since. . .

Slow, Slow, Quick Quick Slow

Whenever the ballroom dancing comes on to the TV my wife sometimes gives a bit of a sigh, and talks about the days when she went dancing as a girl in Belfast, with her dancing shoes wrapped up in brown paper under her arm. And her worrying about whether her father would find out. He thought she was out for a quiet stroll with her chum, the one sitting beside her in the tram, heading for the ballroom.

Up to the end of the Fifties Belfast was a city of ballroom dancers. The Plaza, in Chichester Street, was the biggest dance hall. The top suburban spot was the Floral Hall, at Bellevue, right under the brow of Ben Madigan. Three thousand dancers could have been accommodated in these two places. Another ten thousand could have found a floor to suit their needs among the dozens of smaller halls in the city.

There was great talk of medal dancing in those days. You would hear tell of many a one taking the bronze medal, and much less often somebody you knew would get the silver medal. These were earned at formal examinations, supervised by qualified ballroom dancing experts. The top award, of course, was the gold medal; the winners of that got their pictures in the papers.

My wife was in the medal class as a dancer. During her dancing days she had a partner for competitions. She would change her partner as circumstances dictated, in much the same way as a football manager changes a winger, or a goalkeeper. When I was a young fellow this dancing partner business had me clean baffled, not to say envious. I couldn't even get a girl to say hello to me. The first time I heard one of my mates say that he was going to change his dancing partner I immediately said to him: 'Can I have your old one?'

The ballroom dancing never did appeal to me, though. No harm to the ones who were good at it, but it wasn't my idea of a night out. Brilliantine and patent leather — it definitely wasn't me. I was a pub man. As far as I was concerned Saturday nights were made for sitting in the public bar, arguing the case for the extension of capital punishment to crooked jockeys, amongst other things.

The 1950's had no sooner opened up, however, when, somewhat to my surprise, I found myself taking a girl out on Saturday nights. 'Do you dance?' she wanted to know. 'No' I said. 'Where do you want to go, then?' she asked. 'To the pub,' I said. She decided to join me, but this was only a reconnaisance. 'What do you do with yourself as a rule?' she enquired, as she sipped a dry sherry. 'I drink pints, mostly,' I said, 'and argue about the true meaning of life, or whether it was really an explosion on the island of Santorin that made the Red Sea open that time, things like that.' 'I see,' she said, thoughtfully.

I was working away the next Monday, when the phone rang: 'I've booked a course of dancing lessons for you,' she said, 'private lessons: at Sammy Leckey's dance studio in Royal Avenue.'

'Forward, side, close,' the teacher said. It was the

waltz we were doing. 'Forward, side, close. Don't march, please — dance, on the toes and down again, like this. . .'

'When we're in competitions later on,' the girl said, 'you'll have to learn to smile. By the expression on your face at the minute, you'd think you were getting a tooth out.'

'Slow, slow, quick quick slow,' the teacher said. 'The slow fox trot is the most graceful of all ballroom dances. Wait for your partner to make her turn — don't pull her round like that, we're not doing the Apache dance, you know. . .'

'Right,' the girl said, 'you've a rough knowledge of the waltz, quickstep and slow fox trot. But you've only had private lessons. We'll go to our first dance.' 'Right you are,' says I, 'and don't be surprised if I'm snapped up for the films. I've got one or two variations up my sleeve that'll be the talk of the town by Saturday night.'

In the couple of days preceding my debut I kept dropping references to my mates in the pub. 'I'm taking the woman to a dance on Saturday,' I would say, casually, 'we're practising for the gold medal.' But nobody seemed to be impressed.

I must say I was surprised at the number of people on the floor, when we entered the Plaza. Hundreds of couples were dancing. I was a bit nervous, too. The girl was all done up to the nines, with a proper frock and that. Everybody seemed to know her, as well. When they were greeting her, their eyes would go over me, weighing me up, estimating my dancing standard, I suppose.

Well, they weren't long in finding out. 'What's this dance?' I asked in a whisper, as I held her on a dance floor for the first time. 'It's a waltz,' she said. 'Right,' says I, 'money for nothing. Forward, side, close. Off we go.'

Talk about a shock. I had managed only about three forward side closes when some guy cannons into me. I clean forgot the drill. Somehow I got off again, when somebody else bumps me. That did it. I grabs him. 'How much floor do you need, mate?' I asked. He broke away, fear showing in his eyes. Two minutes later, the same thing: some skinny George Raft type, doing a complicated figure. I complicated him, all right. I was going to knock his head in. 'How do you expect me to remember forward side close, when I'm sent flying in the middle of it,' I said. 'Come on,' said the girl, giving up, 'I can see I'm going to have to develop a taste for dry sherries.'

All the same, I think I had the makings of a dancer in me. When we're watching the ballroom dancing on the TV, I sometimes say that, but it only makes the wife spill her sherry, laughing. . .

When Wee Ned Joined the Order

Out of all the bars I have ever frequented Dempsey's bar down near Donegall Street in Belfast had the greatest collection of characters. There was a big fight manager, a political correspondent, a couple of bus inspectors, and two or three barrow boys from the markets who could be guaranteed to entertain any company; especially Terry McCoy, he was the best practical joker I ever came across. There were some very interesting and amusing ladies got in there too, but we'll not bother about them.

The first time I was ever in Dempsey's — about twenty-five years ago — I fell in with wee Ned Smyth. He was an oxyacetylene burner. He cut up marine hazards for very high wages. He asked me to count up his income tax liability one time and my eyes nearly fell out of my head at the money he was getting. 'I wish I had your brains', he told me, when I finally worked out his assessment. 'Never mind the brains,' says I, 'I wish I had your oxyacetylene burner.'

Well, one day I decided to make an Orangeman out of Ned. It was one Twelfth of July, and the men were just about due back from the field. There was always a lot of them called into Dempsey's: strangers mostly. 'Why is it,' I asked, 'that Orangemen always fold their sashes up in wee brown paper parcels after they've finished walking?'

24

'I didn't know they did,' says Ned. 'Well they do,' I said, 'and if you had a bit of brown paper folded in the same way,' says I, 'you could let on to be an Orangeman just back from the field.'

The idea appealed to Ned. It would be something to report to Terry McCoy in the lounge that night, when the cast were all assembled. We got some brown paper from the home bakery next door: wee Ned had his good suit on, so with the brown paper under his arm he looked the part. 'Try and look tired,' I said, 'you've just walked ten miles, from the field at Finaghy.' We sat there, waiting. Sure enough, before long in the Orangemen started to come, ordering pints as if they'd just been blowing the bagpipes the full length of the Gobi Desert. 'Right, Ned,' says I, 'you're on next,' and out of the side door he went.

It was about five minutes before he came back in. What an entrance! I nearly fell out of my chair. Wee Ned had a black bowler hat on, and he was carrying a pair of white gloves folded in his hand. Alongside him was Bobby Nesbitt, a man I knew for a fact to be a Worshipful Master, a Pastmaster, and every other sort of master you can think of. Bobby was winking over at me: it wasn't hard to see where the bowler and gloves had come from. This practical joke, says I to myself, has taken a sharp turn for the better.

'Give us a couple of buckets of single x,' wee Ned shouts, 'and line up a couple more right behind them,' Bobby Nesbitt puts in, 'for you've got a couple of very thirsty marchers here.'

Gerry Madden the barman was sizing up the house while he took the order, so he didn't actually see wee Ned until he planked the pints in front of him. When he took in the good suit, bowler and gloves I thought he was going to collapse. He backed away as if he had seen a ghost. Wee Ned put the brown paper parcel carefully, no, reverently, on the bar. 'Don't let me walk out without that sash,' says he to Gerry, who could only nod, with his mouth gaping. Even from where I was sitting I could see the whites of poor Gerry's eyes.

Bobby Nesbitt carefully raised his voice. 'That was some flute band, wasn't it, Ned,' he said. 'You're not kidding,' Ned came back. 'Of course,' says he, 'them Scotch bands is all hard to whack: me feet's danced off me.'

From the bottom end of the counter a man I happened to know was in the orange, purple, black and blue wings of the movement shouts up at Ned: 'You were the smartest man on parade,' he says, 'what are you drinking?' 'Thank you most fraternally,' says wee Ned, 'and I'll take a half 'un.'

'I picked you out as soon as you turned into the field,' says another man nearby, 'you really caught the eye; could you manage another one?' 'Could I manage it?' says Ned, 'hit that counter with one and then see what happens.'

Meanwhile, back amongst the spectators I was sitting there trying to puzzle out just why this particular practical joke had turned into such a howling success, but all I could do was shake my head. The whole thing baffled the brain.

A man who was still wearing his chestful of war medals walked up to Ned: 'There you are,' he said, 'for up to now you've been improperly dressed,' and he puts a big orange lily in Ned's lapel. By this time the wee man was away with it. He had definitely no head for the whiskey. He began to sing The Sash My Father Wore. Gerry Madden the barman signalled me over. 'My whole stomach's working in nerves,' he says, 'for dear sake wheel him out before they catch him on.'

Ned, meanwhile, had switched over to The Oul' Orange Flute, and the whole company present was giving him a very enthusiastic hand. But he was due to fold any minute, there was no doubt about that. The same man would be going some if he was able to report on this occurrence to Terry McCoy that night.

I left Bobby Nesbitt's hat and gloves in front of their owner and linked wee Ned outside. Then I propped him up against the wall till I could get his address out of him for the taximan. It was only then, in the daylight, that I spotted it — no wonder the Orangemen had had him taped.

Right there, in his lapel, beside the orange lily, wee Ned was wearing his gold fáinne. 'A Gaelic speaking Orangeman,' says I, 'how are ye.' I could see where the nerves in Gerry Madden's stomach had got their excitement from.

Still, it was a good old day that, in Dempsey's. Maybe some time I'll tell you the one about Terry McCoy and the day he dressed up as a priest.

The Rev. Terry McCoy

Like everybody else, I took everything that Terry McCoy said for gospel, when I first ran across him. He looked so serious, you see, with his thin, studious face, and quiet manner. In actual fact he was the biggest leg-puller I've ever met.

Within minutes he had me believing he was the senior John Jamieson whiskey representative for the whole of Ireland. 'Are you having a drink?' I asked him, feeling quite honoured. 'I'll take a pint,' he said, 'and since you're so courteous, just mention Terry McCoy to the manager and ask him for a complimentary half 'un.'

Very nice, says I to myself, I certainly struck it lucky there. But Gerry the manager paid no attention to the whiskey part of the order: instead he simply handed me the two pints. 'There must have been somebody earywigging,' Terry said, 'if one sees free drink going then they'll all be trying it on. Away round to the side door,' he says, 'knock and explain to Gerry's wife when she answers. Mention my name,' he finished.

'Oh God,' Mrs. Hannigan said, when I'd finished my recitation, 'there's one born every minute,' and she slammed the door in my face.

Somehow I couldn't get annoyed with Terry: nobody ever did.

There was a new barmaid came to work in Dempsey's one time. Terry called her over: 'D'you think that'll affect my livelihood?' he asked, showing her his arm, trembling and shaking something desperate. 'What is your livelihood?' she asked him. 'I'm a signwriter,' he said.

One of his mates wanted to buy him a drink. 'The usual,' he said to the wee new barmaid. 'What's your usual?' she enquired. 'Cheap wine and garlic,' he said, and when the girl said she had no garlic he told her to get some in the usual place. 'Where's that?' she asked. Terry looked to be at the end of his patience: 'In the chip shop next door, where it's always kept, for dear sake,' he said, 'go in there and ask for Terry McCoy's garlic.'

And of course, like everybody else, the barmaid forgave him, after her colour came back to normal.

One day Terry and his mate, Harry Brannigan, were doing a job fixing the boiler belonging to a chapel on the edge of Belfast. Terry had something to do to the radiator in the sacristy, and what does he find hanging up there in a corner but an old cassock, all dusty. Terry gives it a bit of a shake, and, realising there was nobody about, and wasn't likely to be since it was wearing up to lunch time, he put it on, for a bit of a laugh.

He made his way out of the church, chanting and holding his hands up as if he was reading from something. Harry Brannigan didn't know what to think when he saw this priest coming down the steps of the boilerhouse, carrying out some sort of a ceremony. When he spotted who it was the two of them larked about till lunch time. Then, after they'd had their sandwiches, while Harry was marking his football coupon, Terry took a stroll in the grounds adjacent to the boilerhouse, still wearing the cassock.

He was staring absent-mindedly down the street when he heard somebody say: 'Excuse me, Father.' He spun round. There, on the other side of the railings, was Smiler Neeson. Terry beamed at him, in pure delight.

Smiler would neither work nor want. He spent his day tapping winning punters round the pubs and bookies. Since Terry didn't back horses, Smiler didn't know him, but Terry knew your man all right. He looked at him enquiringly, the way he thought a priest would.

Smiler Neeson had earned his name because of the whine in his voice. He advanced close to the railings: 'You couldn't see your way to letting me have a few bob, Father, could you?' he whinged.

Suddenly Terry reached through the railings and grabbed Smiler by the lapels. 'Stand there till I tell you something, Smiler,' he said. Smiler gave a jump when he heard his name, but Terry hung on. 'Last night,' he said, 'I was playing stud poker with some colleagues of the church — and I drew queens and jacks. Everybody packed,' says he, 'except the auxiliary bishop. He bumps the pot and throws four nines at me.' Terry shook Smiler like a rat. 'I'm looking for money myself,' he says, 'how much are you worth?'

Smiler was showing the whites of his eyes. He was looking over his shoulder for an escape route. 'When you've mooched your first quid off the punters,' Terry said, 'bring it up here to me. I want to get the stud poker going again. The choir's due here soon, for practice.' Smiler wrenched himself loose, and took off down the street like a scalded cat. You could have heard Terry laughing at Castle Junction.

That evening, when Terry McCoy was retailing

the story in Dempsey's Bar some punter announced that he had seen Smiler Neeson coming out of a downtown church at two o'clock that day.

Terry slapped his thigh. 'Damn it,' says he, 'if I haven't made my first conversion!'

How To Stay at the Top

I am often asked whether anybody else in the city of Belfast can stand comparison with Francie Spence. My stock answer to that one is No. Or at least if he has a serious rival I haven't run across him yet.

Sometimes Francie Spence reminds me of royalty. He never gets himself involved in argy bargy about his title. There's only one throne, and he's sitting on it. No more need be said. He leaves comparisons to people like me. He's an action man, himself.

How does he stay at the top? I'm asked that too. Dedication, that's how. Give Jack Nicklaus ten minutes to himself, and where is he? He's out there on the putting green, that's where he is. Supposing Margaret Thatcher has half an hour free between meetings — down goes another quango. Or else Russia gets a tongue-lashing.

The top people never relax, you see: that's why they're up there, in the stratosphere. Francie Spence is no different. He happened to be in a customer's house one day when the man from the public assistance called. Many a lesser man would have been out the backyard and over the wall quicker than a rat up a spout. Not Francie. As cool as a cucumber he engages the man in conversation, ignoring the fact that his bucket and ladder for the window-cleaning were sitting at the front door for all to see. Before he had finished he had lodged a claim for the price of warm underclothing through the public assistance. The man promised to expedite the claim for him. 'As you're going out,' Francie said, 'see if you can see that window cleaner. I know he's about, for his bucket and ladder's out there. Tell him this man wants him.'

That's the sort of resource that's needed. He gave me another lesson of the same sort there, not long ago. I walked into the Semi Quaver bar, and there he was, at a table with some stranger. The weather was too bad for the window cleaning; racing at Haydock was abandoned and the only thing going on was the English dog racing. Since no thinking punter takes the English dogs seriously, it was going to be a quiet afternoon.

To my surprise, when I put a bottle of stout in front of each of them and sat down, I noticed that Francie was showing every sign of tension. In fact, tension and strain seemed to be in the air. Barney, the manager, was lying over the bar, taking everything in.

Conscious of the atmosphere, I stayed quiet. Then Francie Spence spoke to the other man at our table: 'Could you not give me a wee bit longer?' he asked. He sounded respectful, even obsequious. I nearly fell out of my chair.

'When you borrowed that twenty sheets off me,' the man said, 'the deal was that you were to pay it back in six weeks, at a fiver a week. The six weeks are up,' he said, 'and you've only paid me twenty. What about the tenner interest? You signed for it.'

He was a stout man, in his forties. His voice was flat, and uncompromising. Francie drew a breath: I could have sworn there was a half sob in it: 'Sure you know how things are,' he said, in a low tone, 'I haven't been near the windows this four weeks, with the weather.' The man shook his head: 'I'm sorry, mate,' he said, 'I've a moneylending business to run. Words'll not pay my overheads.' He pursed his lips: 'I'm going to have to send the van up to your door tonight.'

Francie's eyes widened; his nostrils flared. The whites of his eyes showed clearly. His hand on his glass trembled so much that he very nearly spilled a drop of stout. 'The van!' he cried, 'not that. Not the debtors' van. The one with the writing on it!'

The man smiled, grimly. 'The very one,' he said. Francie Spence's head was bowed. He spoke in a low voice. 'All up and down the side of it in electric lights,' he muttered. 'Bad Debt Recovery Agency'. 'My God,' he said, 'it'll finish the wife: she thinks them days are past. . .' He sat, quiet, shaking his head.

In the pause that followed I tried to collect my thoughts. For one thing, my heart was right down in my boots. An idol was crumbling to dust before my eyes. Was this Francie Spence, the man who had fought off attempt after attempt by the Department of Health and Social Services to get him a job? The man who claimed compensation on the grounds that the constant offers of work by the Department were wearing his nerves out? Was this broken creature before me the greatest expert on National Insurance benefits since Aneurin Bevan kicked the bucket? I felt as though the world had ended in a whimper.

He was sitting there, eyes down, beaten. I was suddenly filled with hatred against the man who had done this to him. I glared at the stranger. He looked at me like Sydney Greenstreet in 'The

Maltese Falcon' except that Sydney Greenstreet didn't have a brown ring round his mouth from the Guinness.

I rose, my mind made up. Opening my wallet, I took out a tenner. I threw it on to the table: 'I mind the time,' I said icily to Sydney Greenstreet, 'when Francie Spence wouldn't have seen you in his road.' Then I turned to go.

To my amazement Francie and his companion stood and solemnly shook hands. With an oath Barney, the manager, turned to the whiskey bottle, and drew them a glass each.

'What do you think of my script-writing?' Francie said, smiling modestly. He pointed to the other man. 'I taught him that act in three minutes.' Since I was still puzzled, Francie explained: 'We bet Barney here that I would get a tenner out of the next man to walk through that door.' With a wink, he gave me back my money.

See what I mean? Whiling away a few idle minutes. . .Nicklaus on the putting green. . .Francie Spence extracting free glasses of whiskey.

Is it any wonder they're at the top?

Funerals Have Lost Their Style

The working classes are in the grip of very severe changes. Take funerals. There's no great distance walked nowadays. Two or three yards for the sake of appearances, then pull in to the side and everybody into the motors.

Of course, some people say that you can't very well have a whole parade of family and friends walking along and causing traffic jams. I maintain that we never should have given way on that one. Flute bands didn't. There's no limit to the number of flute bands that you see out collecting for new instruments or uniforms, and they're not one bit worried about causing traffic jams. The cars can stretch behind them from Carrickfergus to Cork and it's all one to the fluters, and surely if it's good enough for them it's good enough for funerals.

There was something very special about dandering along the road with your hands behind your back, picking away at the man beside you, to see how much you could find out about the ones in front of you. It's not every day you get the chance of a nice leisurely conversation walking along behind the hearse. This goes particularly for family funerals. That second cousin who went away to Birmingham thirty years ago, why has he turned up for this one? Is he sounding the family out, to see who's going to be mug enough to put him up, now that he's ready for the pension? Oh yes, it's how are ye, and many a time I thought about ye, but there's some of us had to bunch up to get the fare for Birmingham for him in nineteen and forty nine, and we're waiting for our money back yet.

There used to be a time when the transport was only needed to bring the men back from the graveyard — you walked the whole road there, and apart from taking your turn with the lift, the journey was hardly noticed, the conversation was that good. Mind you, it was generally slow enough to start with, but once the pace had been established, and you were settled in with your chosen company, away you went, talking and listening, chewing the gossipy bits, remarking on the weather, comparing notes on the horse results with relations from across the water. 'Did you manage to get Monksfield in the Champion Hurdle?' you ask. 'Did I get it?' he'll say, 'sure I was at Cheltenham and saw the race.' 'Get away now,' you reply, 'isn't that great. Actually going to Cheltenham, eh?' And then whenever it's your man's turn for a lift, you say to the one beside you: 'His old fellow was a bit of a blow, and I see where it runs clear down the line.'

Oh aye, there was a great spice about funerals at one time. But what have you now? Walk the length of yourself and you're bundled into a big car, and with my luck, put beside the clergyman more than likely. You'll not hear much inside a motor car; by the time you've finished passing the smokes round you're turning into the cemetery and your chance is over.

And even after you get back it's not the same. If you say you're not staying long everybody looks relieved. I remember the time when you were considered an ignorant plug if you didn't stay between the house and the pub till the small hours of the morning, after a funeral.

I was at a funeral a while ago there. A far out friend. Do you know this? From start to finish of the whole performance there wasn't the slightest indication of trouble in the family. All pals together; christian names and letting on they were the best of friends, when I happen to know that the same crowd were eating each other. In fact, a while back solicitors' letters were on the go.

A funeral was always the time when the like of that came to the surface. Hints and dirty digs all night; references to breeding; remarks like Thank God there's nobody'll be able to say a word about me or my debts when my time comes. Some woman jumping to her feet and saying to her man: 'Get me my coat, for I'll have to go home out of this!' And then, after she's left, everybody saying: 'Sure that one never had any skin on her face. What would you expect from a spinner in the mill?'

It's all gone, the atmosphere. The whole life's away out of funerals. Even if I was to get my way, and I was to walk it the whole road to the cemetery, I would be the only one doing it, for everybody has their own cars now anyway. At this funeral I was at recently, the last remaining relic of family strife was the way a woman would clearly gloat when her man's motor car was better than somebody else's. But of course that's no good. The only one to get any pleasure out of a situation like that's the car owners. Nobody else can join in, the way we did in the old days.

But mind you, you think you're bad till you hear

of somebody worse. Last week old Davy Brady was complaining about the unseemly haste at funerals too. 'I mind the time I could have joined the mourners walking along the street, and didn't even know if the departed was a man or woman. But during the long walk,' says he, 'it was easy to find out, listening to the others around me.' He shook his head. 'Twice a week I could have touched for a drink from people who thought I was a friend of the family. But sure you've no chance now,' he said, 'funerals go a mile a minute. There's no style left in them any more.'

The Poor Loser

I was talking one day to a university lecturer on the subject of philosophy. 'If you were asked to indicate the greatest advantage that your university education has brought you,' I asked, 'what would your answer be?'

It didn't take him ten seconds to reply. And when he did it began with another question: 'Tell me this,' he enquired, 'what kind of a loser are you at the gallopers?'

'Not great,' I said. 'After I've had a bit of a sickener I tend to complain about the grub at home, no matter what it's like.' The university man nodded: 'I know,' he said, 'that's fairly common.' He drew thoughtfully on his pipe. Nearly all university lecturers draw thoughtfully on their pipes. Then he waved it in my face: 'What kind of a loser do you reckon I am?' he asked.

'I can answer that in two words,' I said, 'the greatest.'

And so he is, the same man. I've seen him lose a five time roll-up after a ten-minute wait for an objection, and all he did was take a deep breath and walk over to the Sporting Chronicle to study the next race. Never turned a hair. Definitely the greatest.

'I'm beginning to see what you mean,' I said, 'what you mean is that your deep study of philosophy, and imparting its wisdom to young minds, has given you an inner calm, a stoicism almost, on which you can draw in times of stress.'

He looked at me, puzzled. 'What are you talking about?' he asked. I just shrugged; wrong again. I waited for him to expand on his earlier statement. 'No' he said, 'if university has done any one thing for me it gave me an opportunity to watch Frankie McLaughlin under the stress of a losing bet.' He did the thing with the pipe again. 'Who's Frankie McLaughlin?' I asked. 'He's a visiting reader in law,' your man explained.

'I think I'm with you,' I said, 'This Frankie McLaughlin volunteered to be the guinea pig while you set up an experiment in order to let young minds study the horse betting situation, and the stresses therein.' He gave an exasperated sigh. 'Why do you keep bringing young minds into this?' he wanted to know, 'there're hardly any young minds at university nowadays. Most of the students are in their thirties. They've tried working and it nearly killed them. They're back at university the way a wounded child returns to its mother.'

'Go ahead and tell the story,' I said.

'Your man Frankie McLaughlin was redbrick,' my companion began, 'he had a head as big as Birkenhead about himself. He used to look down his nose at people who played the gallopers especially, until after a while I stopped all mention of the sport in his presence.

'But one day he happened to overhear a couple of customers in a lounge bar talking about a chaser that was out at Newbury. They had county accents and dilapidated tweeds: they definitely looked like men of substance. One was telling the other that a horse called Aristophanes was a certainty, and that he was having a couple of hundred on it. Frankie McLaughlin asked me about it, all excited. "It couldn't beat me," I told him, but he wasn't listening. He was a palpitating mass of nerves.

'Well, I went down to the bookies to have a bit of an interest myself, and to my astonishment Frankie McLaughlin was there: "Did you back Aristophanes?" I asked him. He nodded, but he wouldn't tell me how much he had on it. However, old Paddy McGarrigle told me. He'd overheard the bet being struck, because he'd seen a fiver lying on the ground beside the counter and he'd put his foot straight on top of it. Well, with his rheumatics he wasn't able to bend down to pick the fiver up, and at the same time he couldn't ask anybody else to do it or he'd never have seen it again, so he had to wait for a friendly face, and I was the first one he'd seen. And he'd heard Frankie McLaughlin strike the bet. "Fifty quid," old Paddy said. He'd stuck the fiver on Aristophanes, too, on the strength of it, although as a rule his stake was twenty pence.

'I might as well tell you that I stuck to my judgment,' the lecturer said. 'Even though Aristophanes was being backed like a certainty, I left the race alone.

'Frankie McLaughlin wasn't long in being introduced to the thrills of racing. His horse fell at the last, after leading by half the track. But it was his subsequent behaviour that I really wanted to talk about.

'You talk about losers? In all my life I've never seen a worse one. He actually cried. Imagine a visiting reader in law crying in the bookies. And boy did he send them up. Every punter in the pitch drew away from him in revulsion. "Pull yourself together, old man," I said, "don't let the Light Blues down." But that only made him worse. He ended up clasping the bookie round the knees, and pleading that the fifty quid was needed to pay the Swiss specialist, otherwise the child next door would never walk again. "Would you believe me, mister," the bookie said, "there's not a child in this whole district can walk, if my customers can be believed", and he had Frankie McLaughlin evicted, for creating a disturbance.

'He got the boat to England that night, and I've never seen him since. But do you know this,' the university man said, 'I've never forgotten that lesson. Ever since then I've kept my end up when I'm losing, especially in view of old Paddy Mc Garrigle's splendid example.'

'Oh aye,' I said, 'he lost the fiver that he'd found, didn't he?'

'He did,' said the lecturer, 'and although his eyes watered a bit, there wasn't a tear passed down his face.'

'Sure Aristophanes didn't cost Paddy anything,' I said.

'Did it not?' your man said. 'That's what you think. That fiver had actually dropped out of his pocket in the first place. It was his own money all the time.'

Window Cleaning — The Facts

'Why don't you tell everybody the true facts behind window cleaning?' Francie Spence suggested.

'What I'm thinking of doing right now,' I said, 'is to blatter away at the old Olivetti and see what dances on to the page. I've been thinking a good deal lately of William Butler Yeats and Maud Gonne: then there's your man Wordsworth and that sister of his. You can't whack exploring relationships. There's people has cleared their mortgages out of Yeats and Maud. It's a real Klondyke.'

I summoned the waiter. In Dempsey's bar you do that by holding paper money in the air; cash customers get priority. 'Get Spence a pint there,' I told the waiter, 'and press it well down.' 'What about the scientific stuff, like window cleaning,' Francie said.

'Science,' I thought for a moment. 'Why not?' I mused. 'What about inertial navigation? In the inky darkness of outer space a warhead bigger than the City Hall hurtles at two squillion miles an hour towards its target. Its inertial navigation system ensures that there's no way that the warhead can wander from its preordained course, not even by the thickness of a bookie's docket. . .'

'There you are,' Francie said, 'the horses again, and the bookies. More or less what I expected.'

I stopped stone dead. I felt as if I had been rebuked by Danny Blanchflower for talking too much. 'So it's science, is it?' I said, 'well, since I'm in the company of a senior wrangler, I'd better listen. Something about window cleaning was it?'

'Why don't you turn your attention to window cleaning?' he asked again. I slapped myself on the forehead. 'Of course,' I said, 'what a stupid ass I am, to be sure. Why only this morning the Reverend Ndabiningi Sithole made a broadcast on window cleaning. Senator Edward Kennedy is expected hourly to address the Irish American Caucus on the subject. Window cleaning beats Maud Gonne by half the track, no doubt about it.'

'Do you happen to know what scrim is?' Francie Spence asked patiently. I shook my head. 'Scrim,' I said, 'it's a good word, all right, but no, I don't know what it is at all.'

'There you are for a start,' Francie said, 'well for your information scrim is like the sort of stuff that women used to do embroidery on. It also happens to be the only material that'll clean windows properly.' He went to pick up his pint; then he gave a violent start on finding that it was empty. I held a quid aloft and organised another one. 'If you go to clean a window with the chamois,' Francis went on, 'the housewife is fully entitled to empty your bucket of water over you. Chamois is useless: scrim's what you want, for a scientifically cleaned window.'

'That's it, then,' I said. 'That's the complete story. You've got your title: Window Cleaning — The Facts, and then just the one line: Don't use chamois, use scrim. This is going to be a shortish feature, isn't it?'

'I could tell you stories about cleaning windows that would make your blood run cold,' Francie

45

said imperturbably. I waved an invitation to him. 'How would you like to be twelve feet up,' he said, 'one foot on the window sill and one on the ladder, and suddenly it happens.'

'You feel your trousers splitting?' I suggested.

'No' says he, 'you feel your ladder beginning to cowp on the hard snow and ice.'

'Just while you're on that point,' I said, 'how do you get away with it? You must be the only window cleaner in the western world who has the brass neck to clean windows in snowy weather.' 'Because I tell the customers that I'm selling an all-weather package,' Francie said, 'it's the scientific approach to selling.' 'It's more like blackmail,' I told him.

'Then there's the problem of Government interference in window cleaning,' Francie went on, 'how many people know about that, eh?'

'This government's out to stop all that,' I said, 'civil servants are being driven out of the market place. The dead hand of bureaucracy has no place in a free market. Oh yes,' I went on, 'there'll be cries of anguish, but it'll make no difference. Fresh air will once again blow through the corridors of power.'

'I don't know what you're talking about,' Francie said, 'but what I'm talking about's working the double. Drawing the dole and cleaning windows. That ordinary-looking man walking past your ladder; he could be a double agent, you know, looking out for people doing the double. The next time you might see that man's face,' he said, 'could be in the lower court, when he's doing his best to make sure that you stay for your tea.'

'There wouldn't seem to be any answer to that one,' I said, but I should have known better.

Francie Spence reached into his pocket and pulled something out. Then he put it on. It was a Moshe Dayan eyeshade. 'Would you recognise me now?' he said, with quiet pride. I had to admit that I wouldn't. 'I've a false moustache as well,' Francie said, 'and a ginger wig.' 'Don't show them to me,' I said, 'this place could be stiff with double agents: you might blow your cover.'

I got up to go: 'I'm sorry, Francie,' I said, 'you haven't made your case. It won't do. Window cleaning hasn't got enough dramatic content. You can't expect people to show an interest in such an everyday thing. William Butler Yeats is more the thing. He wrote a very nice poem, but he didn't know much about women.'

'I'll bet you anything you like,' Francie said, 'he didn't know anything about scrim either.'

The Mystery Tour

After the war finished and I got myself settled down again in good old Belfast it seemed to me that it was about time I had a few exciting adventures with our local girls.

According to Harry, the barman in the Waverley Bar, the whole women of the district had lost control of themselves entirely when the Yanks came over. 'Young and old,' he said, 'they all went overboard for the Americans, with their bunches of flowers, and their boxes of chocolate and all that rubbish.'

'Do you think there's any chance of their morals being permanently lowered?' I asked hopefully. Harry snorted. He was permanently off women. Teeshy, his wife, was a real tartar. She even called at the Waverley Bar every Friday morning and collected Harry's wages. Mind you, if Teeshy hadn't done this the wages could easily have gone for a gallop on the horses, but it had firmed up Harry's thinking on Irishwomen. 'It's no good you fancying your chances,' he told me, 'you're no Yank. It's the ring or nothing for you.'

'Oh, there'll be none of that ring lark,' says I, which just shows how young I was. 'You're dead right,' says Harry, 'for d'ye see whenever the banns go up on the church porch — they might as well nail the man alongside them.'

At this stage some stranger at the bar entered

the discussion: 'You can't whack the mystery tours,' he said. Harry and I looked at him enquiringly. 'Take her on a mystery tour,' your man says. He was about my age, and looked as if he generally talked sense. 'Could you just expand on that?' says I. 'This woman,' he says, 'take her on a mystery tour: she's a hundred miles from home and mother. If you can't make headway then,' he finished, 'you don't deserve success.'

I looked at him in admiration. I went further: I bought him a pint.

At eight o'clock a couple of Saturday mornings later I turned up at the bus depot. 'Two for the mystery tour,' I said to this glum looking character behind the window. 'The only mystery about this tour is whether it goes to Monaghan or Clones,' he said, handing me the tickets. 'Either will do, Sunshine,' I told him, for on my arm was a very fair member of the Ulster female resistance movement whose resistance, as far as I was concerned, had only hours to run.

Seated at the back of the bus I said to her: 'Just so long as this destination has a sylvan glade where I can set you on a log and sing Rose Marie, it'll do me.' Her name was Marie, you see. 'If you think I'm going to the Free State to sit on a log with your freezing hands on me,' she said, 'you've another think coming.' 'You'll change your mind when we arrive,' I said confidently. I had a box of chocolates, Yankee style, in my gaberdine coat. That should effect the final push, says I to myself.

'I have an extra twenty quid in my pocket,' I told Marie on the way down, 'and don't let me break into it. It's for a suit length,' says I. 'How're you getting it past the customs?' she wanted to know. 'Wrapped round me,' I said. 'Well mind yourself,' says Marie, 'I heard tell of them selling mashed potatoes in Donegal to people who thought they were buying butter.' I looked at her fondly. It was nice of her to look out for my welfare. By the time we're coming back, says I to myself, you'll be putty in my hands, my girl: I've got you going already.

It was Monaghan we ended up in. 'Come on,' says I to Marie, 'I'll get the suit length first. And then,' I added, giving her a meaning glance, 'we'll get outside of a feed of bacon and egg and black pudding, and then it's you and me for the nearest flowery dell.'

It didn't escape my attention that she wasn't lodging any objection to the idea.

'Give us a brave good suit length,' says I to this young fellow behind the counter in the drapers. 'You want your head examined,' he comes straight back to me. 'Why?' says I, in some astonishment. 'Because,' he said, 'that utility cloth up in the North's as good a material as you'll get anywhere. What you want to do,' he finished, 'is to use some of that money to buy black market clothing coupons up in Belfast and buy your cloth there too.'

'Well,' says I, 'if you don't mind me saying it, that devastating honesty deserves a drink. Are you coming over for one?' 'Hold on,' he says, 'till I get the old fellow down, and I'm your man.'

What a day we had. Talk about entertaining. This man out of the drapers was one of the greatest talkers I'd ever come across, and every word of it worth listening to. We covered the whole course of the war, apportioning blame where it was rightly deserved. We went into the whole ins and outs of boxing, football and rugby. We were agreed that the time was coming soon when every man in the country would have his own aeroplane, and we proved conclusively that there was a God. As well as that we both told Marie that she was the living spit of Jeannette McDonald. I couldn't believe my ears when somebody said it was time to get back in the bus. The mystery tour was over.

I managed to get Marie in the back seat going home. 'If we hadn't met that draper,' I said, 'would you ever have gone into that sylvan glade with me?' 'Sure you know,' she said, 'I would go anywhere with you.' So I gave her the box of chocolates anyway, and then the two of us fell asleep.

A Question of Sport

There was a time there for a while when Dempsey's bar in Belfast was very nearly handed over to the Philistines: it was a near thing all right.

I could see the danger right from the start. One night when things were quiet a stranger called Dunbar suddenly shouted: 'Which welterweight champion of the world has defended his title the most times?'

'Henry Armstrong', about six of us shouted simultaneously, but my heart sank as I was doing it. The sports quizzers had landed in Dempsey's. The enemy was at the gates.

The public house is no place for compulsive quiz masters. They're a complete menace: no matter how hard you try you can't ignore them. For some reason Belfast produces them by the hundred, and always did. I think they were originally spawned round the galleries at the fight bills, not but what they do no harm at the fights: they help to pass the time away while waiting for the slaughter to commence. 'Which welterweight champion of the world came from Sandy Row?', a quiz buff would ask, looking all round him. You scratch your head as if the name's just barely escaping you: 'Mickey Walker', you suggest, only to realize your folly at once. Nobody with a name like Mickey could possibly come from Sandy Row in Belfast. 'Henry Armstrong?' No, he was black. They're all white in Sandy Row. The answer's Jimmy McLarnin, you're told, and you immediately try to salvage some pride. 'Aye, but *when* was he champion?' you ask. '1934', everybody shouts, and you nod your approval, trying to look like Datas, the Memory Man.

Now shift that scene into a public house and I'm telling you, you've got trouble. Start the sporting quizzes and gradually you'll lose all your normal customers. They'll be replaced by walking encyclopaedias who have no conversation except sport. They're only in there for the purpose of doing their turn, trying to ask a boxing question that'll stump the whole house. And I find that I can't resist it. I can't opt out of it. I've seen times when I've been holding the barmaid captive with my scintillating conversation when some voice nearby says: 'Who beat Gorilla Jones of Milwaukee in 1937, and for what title?' Immediately my grip on the barmaid has weakened. The eyes become faraway. Gorilla Jones, eh? It must have been Tony Zale who beat him. But wait a wee minute. Tony Zale was later than 1937. The barmaid's away up to the other end of the bar in disgust: she's being captivated by the pay-out clerk in the bookies. 'I give up!' I shout in frustration. 'It was Freddie Steel', is the answer, and the next thing I'll be sinking a whiskey and chaser in disgust.

The take-over by Dunbar and his followers was quite sudden. Within a fortnight even the Saturday TV racing was no guarantee of immunity. 'The horses are in the stalls,' the racing commentator said. Then: 'Who took the featherweight title of Terry McGovern?' Dunbar shouted, and the TV commentary was lost in the noise of the quiz buffs, all shouting 'Young Corbett!'

'Who was Willie Ritchie?' Dunbar asked. 'An inspector on the buses', I shouted back, trying to shovel some humour on to the proceedings, but I was ignored: 'Lightweight Champion of the World, 1911 and 12', the whole bar seemed to be answering.

"Who holds the record number of Lonsdale belts?' Dunbar wanted to know. 'A moneylender in High Street?' I suggested, but I went unheard. The correct answer was being yelled from the rafters.

'This is getting desperate', I said to Terry McCoy. 'I haven't had a normal conversation in here for three weeks'. He agreed, and between the pair of us we decided to counter attack.

The next Saturday, before Dunbar could lead off with the first of his quiz questions I jumped up on to a chair and addressed the entire clientele: 'Who used to box with silver paper round his waist and a coloured ribbon in his hair?' 'Kid Chocolate', Terry McCoy answered. 'Correct', I said, bowing towards him.

'Name the boxer who has hanged the most opponents', Terry McCoy shouted at the top of his voice. I gave the thunderstruck quiz merchants a couple of minutes, then: 'Benny Lynch', I called out. 'Well done', Terry said.

'Which middleweight champion was covered in stripes?' I asked. 'Dick Tiger', Terry McCoy replied, by which time drinks were being finished up and the quiz brigade were moving towards the door. I stopped Dunbar on his way out. 'Which British boxer had a river running through him?' I whispered into his ear. He pushed past into North Street.

'Brian London', I yelled after his disappearing figure.

Half an hour later we were sitting, steeped in contentment, listening to Big Alex Murray complaining about the Scout's double in the Daily Express, when in walked a wee man with a wispy moustache. He ordered a bottle of stout, took a sip out of it, and then turned to us. 'Who played in six Irish Cup finals and never kicked a ball?' he asked.

'Agnes Street Temperance Flute Band', we shouted, as we threw him into the street.

Pickled Eggs for Luck

I first started going into Dempsey's Bar in the centre of Belfast because Gerry Mulholland recommended it. Dempsey's pickled eggs are very lucky, he said.

What happened to the crème de menthe then? I asked him. Well actually, he said, the pickled eggs took over from the crème de menthe within one crisis-ridden hour.

Now I was interested to hear this. My own lucky charm consisted of blowing my nose twice whenever the horses reached the three furlong mark: it hadn't been too effective lately. I asked the Gerry fellow for full details.

On Derby Day I took time off from the office, he said. I was looking forward to an interesting and maybe profitable afternoon doing the things I liked best — drinking and betting. As well as my own stake money I had carried down about twenty bets on the Derby from a whole load of women in work. You know what women are, he said. I do, says I, they're terrible punters. Well, said Gerry, this list of bets that I had to do was all made up of two bobs and four bobs on big fat outsiders. Picked, says he, because they all had names that were romantic in some way or another, or else they were the same as boy friends or something.

It so happened on this particular day, Gerry

went on, that there was a two-year-old race to open the Epsom meeting. And there was an article in it that looked as if it had been lifted and hurled into the race. In its one and only race beforehand, Gerry explained, it nearly wrecked the clock at Ascot. And mind you, says he, Ascot's rough on you when you're only a two-year-old, as you know fine well, without me telling you.

That's one of Gerry Mulholland's characteristics: he identifies utterly and completely with the horses that he backs. One of our mates, Sammy Fry, maintains that, if you timed it right, and waited till one of your man's TV selections was in the winner's enclosure getting rubbed down, you could hand Gerry a handful of hay and he would eat it, and give your hand a bit of a lick along with it.

Now, says Gerry, this thing in the first race at Epsom looked as if it could lose a hoof and still win slowing up. So naturally, he says, I emptied the lot on, at four to six.

The lot? I asked, meaningly. The lot, he said, including all the bets the women had sent down out of work for the Derby.

Merciful and true heavens above and the earth beneath, I said, not to mention the waters under the earth. You should know, and none better, never to lay a woman's bet. Lovely Cottage in the Grand National — romantic name: Sheila's Cottage — ditto: My Love — ditto: all winners at huge prices. Husbands and brothers all over the British Isles nearly bankrupt because they didn't bother going near the bookies with such ridiculous bets.

Oh, I know, I know, Gerry said, but the man who never made a mistake never made anything. After I placed the bet, he went on, I had the usual crème de menthe for luck; in the Semi Quaver Bar;

raising it to my head right on the off; closing my eyes and drinking it from the wrong side of the glass the way I always did for crucial bets.

I take it, says I, that the hot pot was hammered? Hammered? he repeated, I don't think that horse ever finished the course. It's probably still drifting around the Epsom Downs like the Marie Celeste. Either that, or its mouldering skeleton's still in the starting stalls. Gerry sat silent for a minute: then he went on.

I stumbled out into High Street like a drunk man. Talk about being stunned! I had exactly six bob left, Gerry said. I needed eight quid just to cover the bets from work. And if any of them connected — curtains!

I walked about till just before the Derby went off, then I found myself in Dempsey's bar. To give myself a bit of an interest in the race, he said, I backed the biggest outsider in it; it was a horse with a completely unromantic name: Psidium, it was called. I had five bob straight on it: that left me with a shilling.

Go no further, says I, go no further. You bought a pickled egg with the shilling, right? Wrong, he says, I bought two pickled eggs with the shilling. I ate one before the off, and the other one during the race. And what a race, he said, his eyes shining.

Psidium — a sixty six to one winner, I said, I envy you, definitely.

It was the pickled eggs, Gerry said, modestly.

And do they still do the trick? I asked him.

Oh, they're lucky enough, Gerry Mulholland said, the pickled eggs are lucky enough, I've no complaint there. What does get me down, says he, is the barium meal tests, every three months.

In Clubland

Years ago I used to go into a working man's club in East Belfast on a Sunday morning for a contemplative drink before Sunday dinner. Somehow that drink always had a special attraction over and above the one in an ordinary pub.

The licensed trade didn't fancy the clubs, of course, and still don't, in the North. But while they were lobbying public representatives for Sunday opening of pubs all I was interested in was stopping my head from opening and closing as a result of Saturday night's carry-on. It was all the same to me where the drink was being sold on a Sunday morning: if necessary I would have swum Belfast Lough from Antrim to Down, and there was any amount like me.

Just before noon — opening time — I would be standing discreetly in a convenient gateway near the club. There wouldn't be a sinner as far as the eye could see. Just the usual Belfast Sunday, with the labouring population lying in bed stunned: fish and chip papers, and beaten racing dockets swirling along the pavement, and maybe an old dog nosing the lid off a dustbin. Then the first stroke would belt out from the Albert Clock, and that's when the miracle happened. It never failed to stop me dead when I witnessed it.

People appeared from everywhere. From cracks in the tiles, up out of street gratings, down the spouts, out of the sky. If my convenient gateway was only twenty paces from the club door, and if I'd started walking towards it at the first gong, I found to my astonishment that I was at the back of a queue that was double and triple banked. Ahead of me, nervous to get in, were dozens of drinkers with the undoubted ability to become invisible at will.

And they all had that same hunted look about them — an expression that told you that all they wanted to do was to get off the streets tout' suite: get inside that lovely, gloomy, friendly club, and relax among kindred souls, before they were captured by some passing missionary, and hauled into church to answer charges.

Once inside, although there was some easing of the strain, that wary appearance stayed with them until they were actually at the table, and the first, healing mouthful was on its way down. Then you could see shoulders coming down, backs settling against chairs; you could hear sighs of sheer gratitude. It was then that the customers would begin to recognise each other; nods would be exchanged; good mornings would be said. And when tongues were able to get round words again, the conversation would start. The true joy of the Sunday morning session would begin.

One of my favourites was a character named Scotty. He used the club to ventilate an ongoing complaint about his wife Martha: 'She can't read, you see,' he would explain, 'and it wouldn't be so bad if she would just keep off the subject. But no. Whenever there's a visitor in our house Martha has to let on she can read. Nobody has mentioned reading, but she has to bring it in.' Scotty would roll his eyes in despair and lower three quarters of a pint, while he brought himself under control. 'She'll lift the Belfast Telegraph,' he would go on, 'then she'll say something real daft, like: I see where the Lord Major was in the City Hall yesterday. She can't pronounce things either,' he would finish, dejectedly.

I may say that Scotty, too, had his own ideas as to expressing himself. Retailing a yarn to me once about a court appearance he'd made, it turned out that he addressed the RM as 'Your Magistrate.' And when he was looking more brightly on Martha than usual, he said maybe it was just a phrase she was going through.

I met a young lad in the club for a lot of weeks who was going through a bad patch at the horses. As well as everything else he'd lost the few quid he was supposed to give to his mother for his keep. 'I told her I've been promoted to charge hand in the factory,' he said, 'and that I've been put on to monthly pay.'

Three weeks later the luck was no better. 'That's a month you owe your Ma,' I said, 'what are you going to do?' 'I've already done it,' he said, 'I told her I'm the manager now, and they're paying me quarterly.'

Once the club filled up it was an education to see the waiters in action. To the man used to an ordinary pub, the sheer scale of the demand would have had him gaping in astonishment. There was a vast membership, and by one o'clock they all seemed to be present, with their brothers and cousins as well. When the waiter went to the counter it wasn't a matter of two beers and a lager please. Not at all. Each waiter had a sort of bakeboard, with dozens of holes, large and small, drilled into it. Putting his bakeboard up on the bar, the waiter would yell something like: 'Twenty two pints, fourteen bottles, and nine half 'uns.' When the bottles and glasses were fitted into their special holes, away he would stagger through the crowd, with what I would call a decent, manly order by any standards.

Since Sunday morning was for curing sore heads it was to be expected that the club was the place to go, to see the better class of hangover. The choicest one I ever saw was the property of a man who came into the club on Christmas morning, about twenty years ago, as a sudden fall of snow came on. He sat down at a table with his drink, and it so happened that his table was underneath an open window.

The wind shifted, and strengthened, and snow flurries began to blow in through the window, but this fellow paid no attention: he just sat there, woodenly, staring at his drink. As the rest of us in the vicinity watched in fascination the fat snow-flakes plopped on top of his head and his shoulders. His hair became a Father Christmas wig, and the snow was three inches deep on his lap: it dusted his eyebrows, and it melted and ran down the side of his nose, but he never moved a muscle. He sat impassively, as he changed before our eyes into a snowman.

'Brother,' I said to the man beside me, 'that's some prizewinning hangover.'

'I just wish I had the half of what it cost,' he said, in awe.

Sometimes, whenever I got back from the club and was settling down to the Sunday dinner, the missus would say to me: 'Honest, I don't know what you see in that old club.'

Well, if she sees this, she'll know now.

Francie Spence and the Holiday Pay

Every time I complete another section of Francie Spence's biography it strikes me that he's like a stick of rock — he's got a core of pure history that runs right through him, no matter how far back you go.

You've heard about the infant whose future was pre-ordained — he emerged from the womb with the midwife's gold ring in his hand? Well, it won't surprise me in the least if that infant turns out to be Francie Spence. I have investigated him at a great many stages in his development, and every single exercise has turned up some example of that special quality that singles him out from ordinary men. He never stops making history.

I have now reached the year 1937 in my researches: the wee man was nearly fifteen at that time. Since he had left school less than a year before he had been sacked from a foundry, a shipyard, a flax spinning company, Belfast Corporation Roads Department, and a leading turf accountant's. He was sacked from the first four jobs for backing horses during working hours. In each case he put up the perfectly reasonable argument that horse racing takes place during working hours, for goodness sake, and when else was he to do his betting? He lost his case each time, and he felt very aggrieved about it. That's how he came to apply for the job in the bookie's, marking the results up on the board. Surely to God, he argued, they can't fault me for backing horses during working hours now. They might as well sack a baker for buying one of the firm's crusty loaves: that's the way Francie saw it.

But no. He was emptied out of the bookies as well. And when he used the crusty loaf analogy the manager of the pitch shook his head. 'It won't do'. he said. 'Marking the horse that you backed up as the winner, irrespective of whether it won or not, is not the same as buying the crusty loaf. It's the same as shoving cakes and buns up your jumper, and smuggling them out, that's what it's the same as.'

So he got a job in a small wareroom, parcelling up the newly made shirts, and delivering them to wholesalers. It got him out and about. He was able to keep in touch with the sport of kings, and really, since he was too young to drink, there was very little else that Francie asked of life than that.

It was one of those firms, so numerous in the 1930's, where the employees worked for next to nothing and thought they were lucky to have such a considerate boss. One day the considerate boss sent for Francie. 'I would just like you to know that I'm well pleased with you,' he said. He smiled at him. 'You know what happens tomorrow, don't you?' he asked. 'I do,' says Francie, 'it's the Ascot Gold Cup.' 'No', says his boss, 'tomorrow we break up for the holidays.' Again he smiled at the wee fellow. 'I'm giving you your week's holiday pay,' he said. 'Oh, thank you very much,' Francie said, pleased. 'Yes,' says the boss, 'you can draw fourteen shillings instead of seven'. Very nice, says Francie to himself, I can have a nice wee bet with fourteen bob. 'Of course,' the boss said, 'I'll have to recover the extra pay from your wages at a shilling a week when you get back, but sure you'll never miss it.' Francie shrugged. It was an interest-free loan, at worst, and seven extra shillings on the winner of the Gold Cup, at best.

Next day Francie drew the fourteen smackers at lunch time. Instead of waiting until later for the Gold Cup, he shoves the lot on a first-time runner in a two-year old opener. It was hammered by two lengths. Francie walked slowly and pensively back into work. His fellow workmates were laughing and singing at the thought of being off for a whole week with pay. Francie's gloom was noticed at once. 'What's the matter?' they asked. 'I lost my two weeks' pay. . .' Francie began. He never got the chance to tell them how he had lost it. 'The wee lad's lost his pay,' they shouted, 'get the boss.' 'He's a very good man,' they explained, 'he's sure to help you.'

The boss was all concern. 'Where did you lose it?' he wanted to know. Francie nodded in the direction of McKelvey's pitch, 'out there,' he said. 'Out of your pocket?' the boss asked. Francie felt justified in nodding yes. 'Right,' the boss said, 'I'll help you.' 'What did we tell you,' his employees all said to Francie. 'What I'm going to do,' the boss said, 'is to organise a whip-round. You're not going to see this wee lad stuck, are you?' he asked the work force. 'Yes,' they shouted back, but the innate kindness of their employer won the day, and Francie was presented with another fourteen bob from his comrades, just in time for him to shove it on to the winner of the Ascot Gold Cup at seven to two. The actual amount he lifted was three guineas.

Holding on to the odd three shillings — for he had a certain amount of prudence — Francie crammed the three quid on a horse named Brasso, figuring it was about time he cleaned up. Brasso won at six to four: he now had seven and a half sheets, plus, of course, the three bob reserve. He was ever mindful of his mother, so he promised himself that, come what might, he would give her the three bob. Then he lashed the seven and a half on Gordon Richards, who duly obliged at evens. Francie Spence had fifteen pounds. He was making Phoenix look bottom heavy.

He went back into the wareroom and gave his workmates the fourteen bob that they'd chipped in for him. As he was describing his run of luck the boss came in and overheard him. 'You're sacked!' the boss yelled, 'I want no gamblers here. Get out!'

Francie departed, whistling. 'Imagine whistling, when you've just lost your job,' the boss shouted after him, angrily.

Francie stopped and looked back. 'I'm not whistling for that,' he said, 'I'm whistling because, just before you sacked me, I was going to pay you back that seven bob I owe you.'

The Price of Dishonesty

One Monday a long time ago — well, the pint was
two shillings, that's how long ago it was — George
Magee and Harry Morrison were sitting upstairs in
a Belfast trolley bus, coming from work. They
were sitting in total silence, the pair of them.
George Magee was in total silence because a malig-
nant fate had robbed him of twelve pound six the
previous Saturday.

He had done three doubles and a treble at the
horses. The first one lobbed at evens and the second
one at seven to four. When the third one touched
at five to one George sat in Dempsey's bar bragg-
ing and showing people his docket instead of
shooting into the bookies and lifting the £.s.d.
immediately. He was careless and he paid for it,
because, by the time he went in to collect his
winnings, a steward's enquiry was under way.
The five to one shot was eventually rubbed out
and George Magee got twenty-two shillings instead
of thirteen pound eight.

That's why he was silent in the bus that Monday
evening.

Harry Morrison was just naturally the silent
type. He never showed his hand. There was one
day seven of us all took the afternoon off work to
back a horse called Bald Eagle in the Two Thousand
Guineas. We were expecting this article to pay our
expenses in Dempsey's bar for the day. Since it

was odds-on we all had a right go at it. But it wasn't to be.

Bald Eagle was beaten that day by a horse name of Pall Mall. It came in at a hundred to eight. I'm telling you Dempsey's bar was like a funeral parlour.

'This is the worst day for Ireland', I said to Harry Morrison, 'since Cromwell hit Drogheda'. 'It is', says he, 'will you excuse me?' and he got up to go. 'Don't do anything foolish', I said. 'I won't', he assured me. And he certainly didn't, for what he actually did — and I have this from an eye witness — was to slip into the bookies next door, lift twenty seven and a half quid off a two pound bet he had on Pall Mall, and then vanish, leaving the seven of us in Dempsey's steeped in gloom.

So Harry wasn't a one to say anything anyway.

This Monday the two boyos were practically skinned. Harry had four bob and George had nothing. Harry had offered to buy George a drink, so they were sitting in the trolley bus heading for Dempsey's to have that one solitary drink, and wishing it would run to a couple more. Suddenly Harry nudged George in the ribs and pointed to where some guy with a tin of paint in his hand was taking his seat across the gangway from them. George glanced over, then he came alert.

On the floor at the newcomer's foot there was a pound note lying. The two boys sat riveted, watching that pound like pointing gun dogs. The other fellow collapsed into his seat, bent down to put his tin of paint on the floor and then he, too, spotted the oncer.

He stiffened as well, and glanced around. But by that time George and Harry were peering intently

out of the bus window at a wall poster that said
'Ah — Bisto!' They were examining that poster as
if it was the Mona Lisa. When they looked across
the bus again your man had put the tin of paint
on top of the pound note.

George and Harry nodded to each other. It was
more or less what they would have expected. 'Of
course', George whispered to Harry, 'with my
luck, *we* couldn't have picked that seat, could
we?' But Harry just smiled quietly, and tapped
the side of his nose with his finger.

One stop before Dempsey's bar the passenger
opposite bent down, picked up the paint, and the
pound note, and got to his feet. 'Come on', Harry
Morrison whispered, rising as well. The two of
them jumped on to the street and the bus pulled
away.

Walking up Donegall Street right behind the
other fellow, George Magee said: 'Life's funny,
isn't it? Some people get the breaks and some
people don't. Take that fellow there with the
paint. He doesn't need two or three pints the way
I do. I'll bet you whatever you like he wants that
pound to buy more paint or something. A
shilling'll get you a thousand pound he doesn't
know what disappointment is. That man there
has never known the trauma of losing twelve
pound six because of a steward's enquiry.' By
this time George Magee was really worked up.
'I've a good mind', says he, 'to pour that tin of
paint all over him!' But Harry Morrison just looked at George and winked.

Then he hurried forward and tapped the man on
the shoulder. 'Excuse me', he said, 'did you just
find a pound note?'

Well, the man with the paint nearly collapsed.

69

He went red, white and blue. 'Yes' he said, 'yes, yes, I did'. Harry Morrison said nothing, just held his hand out. 'Here y'are', the man said, pressing the pound note into Harry's hand — indeed acting as if he would contribute more than that, if anybody was to ask him. 'Thanks', Harry said, and he and George walked into Dempsey's bar and ordered two pints with that certain ease and confidence that indicates in a man that he's not one bit worried who joins the company.

After George had annihilated the first pint he turned to Harry and smiled:

'Your man with the paint'll be kicking himself by this time', he said.

'Waste no salt tears on the likes of him', Harry Morrison replied, 'for dishonesty is always found out in the end'.

The Pen Pals

I saw an old-timer making his way down High Street in Belfast a couple of days ago, and he put me straight in mind of old Paddy McGarrigle. He was walking as if he was a puppet on a string, all disjointed and floppy — just the way Paddy used to lurch along.

Of course it couldn't have been him, he's been dead these twenty years, but it certainly got me thinking about him.

Paddy McGarrigle sold papers near the City Hall for years, then the rheumatics put him off the street altogether. After that he would have been seen in Dempsey's bar on the evening of his pension day. For the rest of the week he disappeared. I think he just sat alone in his wee dark room in Albert Street and waited for pension day to come round.

I first got to know him when he tipped me an eight to one winner called Scalded Cat. He was standing next to me at the bar, all jerks and tremors, watching me studying the next race. 'Back that one', he said, pointing at the runners in the paper, 'it'll not be bate the day'. His finger was trembling all over the place, but it settled on to Scalded Cat, a horse about three runners down the list. I had a few bob on it and gave old Paddy something of the proceeds. 'Didn't I tell you the top weight would win', he said triumphantly.

'But it wasn't top weight', I said. 'Ach', says Paddy. 'you backed the wrong one; that old finger of mine wouldn't keep still. I was trying to point out the top horse in the list. Sure I wouldn't know its name'. 'Well, anyway,' I replied, 'you staggered on to a winner, so never mind.'

We got along famously. He used to keep me greatly entertained, giving me the scandal about the quality people of Belfast. 'You see it all from a paper stand,' he said, 'never mind the world and his wife — I used to see the world and his fancy woman. Newspaper sellers are like lamp posts,' he explained, 'they're never noticed'.

I'll not pass on any of the stories old Paddy told me about the quality, and their goings on. Let sleeping dogs lie. In any case most of the subjects are dead with Paddy, God rest him. But something just as interesting was the brief flurry of correspondence that arose between Paddy Mc Garrigle and his old mate Con, another paper seller, whose second name I've forgotten.

Con and Paddy had been a long time in the City Hospital together. Paddy got better, but Con was still in there. 'I got a Christmas card from Con', Paddy told me, 'I would love to send him one back'. 'Well why don't you?' I asked him. 'Because I can't read or write', Paddy explained. 'Sure, that's easy fixed', I said.

'Dear Con', I wrote on the best of stationery. 'So pleased to get your card. Things are pretty humdrum around town at present. Everybody seems well-behaved. What's Belfast society coming to? Will write again soon. Kindest regards, Paddy'.

'Oh ho', Paddy chortled, 'that'll not half shake him. Old Con'll fall out of bed with the shock. Things are pretty humdrum'. He roared and shook till his joints reminded him of the liberty he was taking. It was probably the first time in his life that he had ever been a winner. 'That's one up for McGarrigle', he said, 'just wait till Con gets that read out to him'. 'Why', says I, 'can he not read either?' 'Divil the bit of him', Paddy said, 'that's what annoyed me about getting the Christmas card from him'.

But Paddy and I both had a surprise coming. Next pension day he made his way towards me with his rag doll's wobble. 'Read that out to me', he said, handing me a letter. 'Dear Paddy', it said. 'So grateful for your note, including the society bulletin. Please keep writing. After all, as Aristotle said: "What is a friend, but a single soul dwelling in two bodies?"'

'God take care of us', says I, 'who's the ghost writer?' 'I don't know', says he, 'but don't let him away with that'.

'Dear Con', I wrote, 'my good, Aristotelian friend. How aptly you express our relationship, for you and I are all that are left of a once teeming crowd. As Matthew Arnold so touchingly put it: friends who set forth at our side falter, are lost in the storm: we, we only, are left'.

'That should put him in his place', I told Paddy, as I licked the envelope. But I didn't tell him about my postscript. 'PS', I had written, 'whoever you are, if it's war you want, I'm your man. I am armed with a dictionary of quotations. I also know a woman who works in the Central Lending Library. So knock it off with the Aristotle, or else. OK?'

Next pension day: 'Dear Paddy. The old finger joints are not what they were, so I'll not be writing again till about next Christmas. Look after yourself, and mind your company. Con'.

PS. 'Matthew Arnold also said that men of culture are the true apostles of equality. I thought at first that you, whoever you may be, were a man of culture, but it turns out that you're only an ignorant plug. Keep your dictionary, and your woman in the library too, for I want nothing more to do with you'.

'Do you know what that amounts to?' I asked Paddy, when I'd read out the body of the letter only. 'That', says I, 'is an instrument of surrender'.

'Did we bate him them?' old Paddy asked, anxiously.

'Game, set and match', says I, 'let's drink to you and Matthew Arnold.'

Sports Report

I used to report the soccer for an English paper for years. I did it from about 1955 until about 1965: never missed a Saturday during all those seasons.

Every writer should serve some time at it. The training's priceless. I've seen me actually up on my feet in the press box, ready to run for the only telephone on the street outside, with the score at nil each, and only seconds to go: my two hundred words written and ready, the referee looking at his watch, and right out of the blue somebody sticks the ball in the onion bag and you've suddenly got a result. And then, of course, the whistle goes.

'If ever a match ended fairly and squarely this one did', your report runs, 'not even for ten consecutive seconds in the whole ninety minutes did either set of forwards look like piercing the opposing defence. Yet, with it all, a draw was a fair result: indeed it was an inevitable result. . . .' And so on, and so on. You're still running helter skelter to grab the telephone, taking the steps in the grandstand three at a time, but you're composing like mad as you're running.

'If ever a match *looked like* ending fairly and squarely this one did!' you mutter to yourself, as you elbow the Belfast Telegraph out of your way, 'only for about ten consecutive seconds right at the end of the ninety minutes, did any set of forwards look like piercing their opponents' defence, and in the end it was the Reds who did it. Yet, with it all, this was a fair result: indeed, it was an inevitable result. . .'

With this sort of experience you get, after a while, to be so expert that you can prepare a draft match report that looks like a government form. 'Crusaders-stroke-Cliftonville can only blame themselves for losing these points. Thompson-stroke-McKee had his chances, heaven knows, and if it had not been for the catlike grace of Armstrong-stroke-Johnston in the Crusaders-stroke-Cliftonville goal the winning margin would have been much greater than one-stroke-two-stroke-three. . . .'

In my case I very much regret to say that the match report was strongly influenced by the horse results. I had this routine, you see, of nipping into the bookies on arrival in the town where the match was taking place, and having a bit of a mow in one of the races. The outcome of that race dictated the mood of the piece that was phoned over to Manchester later.

Forty shillings down the drain at Newbury and there was no way that any of the two sides were going to get fulsome praise out of me. 'It was said here that a scout from West Bromwich Albion was watching this match. Well, if there was, all I can say is that he must have come to the Showgrounds to get out of the rain. He certainly couldn't have come to see the football. After all, what is there in the record of either of these sides to indicate that they know how to find goals?. . .' and furthermore, I felt like writing, this town has got to be just about the unluckiest one in the entire north of Ireland. Every time I set foot in it I seem to give the bookie forty shillings. . .

But there was the other side of the coin. I remember doing a match in Coleraine one time, and I misread the bookie's board. I thought a horse called Hit The Pace was favourite so I placed my thirty bob on it. It won, and then I discovered that it was ten to one.

'There has been criticism of the home side,' I wrote, 'and it has also been suggested that their opponents lack penetration: never has judgment been more unfair. On their day — and it was my good fortune to choose their day — these teams can put on a display of football that can only be described as the sheerest artistry. Mind you, it was a day for good football, mild, with a gentle breeze. . .' and, I was itching to add, an oul' ten to one shot up on the board, over and above the match.

There is a wonderful camaraderie amongst soccer reporters. One Christmas morning at the traditional Steel Cup final in Belfast for 'B' League sides, I needed as much as I could get.

There was a goalmouth mix-up and the ball hit the back of the net. None of us was too sure as to the scorer. It was coming up to half time: 'I'll go down to the dressing room on the whistle, and ask the players,' I volunteered.

As I went through the door of the pavilion an official took my arm, and said: 'Would you like a drink?' I looked at him in astonishment. Soccer officials aren't exactly given to this sort of gesture towards reporters. I noticed that this one was eyeing me with considerable respect: clearly I was being mistaken for someone else. I nodded, and allowed myself to be led to a cupboard. The man opened it, and left me to it. Inside were rows and rows of glasses of whiskey.

It was a bitterly cold day. I knocked one back smartly, before I was nailed. It really was cold. I took another. The official was talking to someone, who was pointing to me, and shaking his head vigorously. I demolished a third glass and left, nodding pleasantly in face of the angry glances of the two at the door.

By the time I got to the press box I was singing 'Jingle Bells.' 'Did you get the scorer?' I was asked. 'No' says I, 'but I got six half 'uns. Who cares who scored the goal,' and away I went again with 'Jingle Bells.' My colleagues raised their eyes to heaven and one of them took my notebook, with a sigh.

Next day, nursing my hangover, and wondering what sort of whiskey it was, I read my match report. I must say I enjoyed it. The guy who wrote it was a better reporter than I was. He was certainly a soberer one, on the day.

Father's Christmas Party

My father first went to sea as a boy, in 1897. He made his final voyage in 1951, and in all those 54 years he was only twice home for Christmas. The first time was during World War One, when, according to Mother, Tiger's Bay, where we lived, became noisier than the Western Front. He was a sergeant major in the army then, and if I'm asked how a donkeyman greaser in the merchant service came to be a sergeant major I'm bound to say that I'm not too sure. His own explanation was that he worked in the Cunarder 'Olympic' at the time: it was a troopship under army command, and as donkeyman greaser my dad claimed that he automatically assumed army rank in keeping with his position as leading hand in the engine room. This could be true, but my dad was a bit of a character in his straight-faced way. For all I know he could have been impersonating a sergeant major. In any case, I wish I'd seen him in the uniform, he was only five feet four and about as wide as your finger. I'll bet the genuine soldiers stopped in their tracks and scratched their heads when they saw him in the street, with his Western Ocean roll, and the hands jammed into his pockets.

Well anyway, apart from the faces that Mother made when that wartime Christmas at home was mentioned, I knew nothing more, and the older I got the more I used to sympathise with Dad as one Christmas after another came around, and his present was dispatched to him by parcel post weeks before the date. 'Merry Xmas, Daddy,' we used to write, round about the 4th of December. It seemed such a shame.

He wasn't a man much given to talking yet he did plenty of talking abbut that: 'I'm going to miss Christmas again, sweetheart,' he used to say to Mother, and she would say aye, it's awful isn't it, but away in behind her sorrowful glance I used to imagine I could see the ghost of a glint of gratitude, almost thanksgiving.

Now when I was a young man, I was, of all the family, the one who spent most time in Dad's company when he was at home. This is not because I had any more special relationship than the other brothers had with him: no, it was because the brothers had things to do outside of drinking pints, and I hadn't, and when Dad was at home he became unsettled and nervous if he had to sit around the house for any length of time. 'Throw on your coat and come on,' he would say to me in the mornings, and in the afternoons and in the evenings. 'Where are we going?' I would ask. 'We'll take a bit of a dander and get the fresh air,' he would say. About a minute and a half later the two of us would discover, to our surprise, that we had landed up outside Jimmy McGrane's pub in Spamount Street, and in we would go, to get out of the cold. It was only to be expected therefore that Dad's second Christmas at home should leave its mark on me, more so than anybody else.

It was 1950, a year before I was married, and a year before Dad died and was buried in Cuba. There were just the three brothers, the sister and myself at home, for Mother was four years dead then. Father's ship tied up in Immingham in Yorkshire a week before Christmas, and he wasn't due to sail until the 27th. 'Right Sam,' he said, the minute he hit Belfast off the Liverpool boat, 'you and me have to stock up for the Christmas party.' 'Where are we having it?' I asked. 'In the parlour,' he said. We called in for a jar on the way home from the boat, and when I left I was humping a dozen of stout, the first of the special party stock. After the sister had coaxed him into eating a wee pick of fried ham and a cup of milky tea, round to Jimmy McGrane's we went: 'I'm going to be home for Christmas,' Dad said to all his cronies, 'and I'm throwing a party.'

At first I wrote down the names of the acceptors, but no paper could have held out to it. 'We're going to need some drink for *this* party' I told him. 'Right then,' he said, 'go up to the bar and get some,' and with that he thrust a handful of mint-fresh notes at me. On the 22nd, 23rd and 24th of December our parlour began to look more and more like Jimmy McGrane's. There was drink everywhere. The sister wasn't too sure what to do about it all. For all our lives we'd been used to Dad just going round for a mouthful, and coming back like a gentleman — sometimes an unsteady gentleman, but well under control for all that — and now things seemed to be heading for an unmerciful binge, and in the parlour too, a place reserved for the clergyman, or maybe the insurance man, if he was paying out on a policy.

'Do the parlour up a bit,' Dad said, 'make it look like a bar.' So I put a lick of paint on it, and rigged up a makeshift bar out of a sideboard and a china cabinet, covered with curtain material.

'Right,' I said to Dad on Christmas Eve morning, 'the bar's all ready, we've enough drink for the First Battalion of the Rifles: what time does the party start?'

'Midnight,' he said. I gaped at him. 'Well,' says he, 'the pubs'll be open till ten, and we usually bring a carry-out, don't we? So it'll be midnight before we finish our normal drinking. I've told the guests to arrive at twelve, and to prepare for an all-night session.' 'How old are you now?', I asked him. 'Sixty-eight,' he said. 'Excuse me for asking,' I said, 'but what did your mother feed you on?' 'I don't see what you're driving at,' he said, and so help me God he didn't.

They came from far and near to Dad's Christmas party, and every blessed guest brought a bottle. Standing behind the bar, I tried desperately to get them to take the drink we'd left in, but the stock actually grew larger as the morning wore on. I heard Dad reminisce with old pals he hadn't seen for years upon years. 'Do you mind the time we rolled the hundredweight of cheese down the gangway at one in the morning?' one old seadog said. 'Aye, I do,' Dad said, 'that was in Cork. We sold it to a publican for a bottle of whiskey.'

It was a lovely party: a delightful party. They were standing on top of each other, singing songs, and weeping and shaking hands. When it finally came to an end at dawn, seven or eight of the guests had to be carried and laid out on sofas or beds. And dad was as steady as a rock. And as happy as he could be without my mother.

On Boxing Night I left him down to the Liverpool boat. 'What on earth am I going to do with all that liquor in the parlour?' I asked him as we shook hands.

'What do you usually do with liquor?' he asked, 'you drink it, don't you?'

And away he went to sea, at 68 years of age. Five feet four, and seven stone ten. The quart into a pint pot champion of the world.

The Wild Dog Rover

In the year 1929 the women of Tiger's Bay in North Belfast must have been pretty close to cancelling Christmas.

Nearly all their menfolk were on the streets. The shipyards were both going bad. The dole had been cut down, and that's where it hadn't been cut off entirely. Men, some of them with the best of trades, were on the outdoor relief, concreting the streets, for a few shillings a week.

I remember seeing them, as a kid of eight, hoking the kidney pavers out of the road with crowbars, and throwing them into a mechanical stonebreaker. Then they threw the crunched up chippings into the concrete mixer and spread the concrete itself over the road. The whole operation was finished off by dropping a heavy plank edge-wise on the concrete, inch by inch, to level it. The levelling just outside our house was done by Bobby Walker's old man, partnered by a man from the bottom of the street called Scanlon, who was slightly gassed at the Somme.

A taxi used to come up the street to deliver the pay. When the men were lined up, and the money was being doled out, the women at their doors, and the watching kids, used to stare in silence, their gazes fixed on the silver and notes, their mouths open, slowly and absently licking their lips.

Somehow my mother dug up a penny apiece for me and my four brothers and one sister. My dad was a seaman, stranded ashore, his ship, like thousands of others, under the command of a watchman at the quay. But on Christmas morning I was out on the street from eight o'clock, with my penny, and a thing that unrolled and made a scraking noise when you blew it. I was joined by our Jim and Frankie Pattison, and Butler Forsythe. Each of them had some wee thing, plus a copper. Then Alec Reynolds came out. 'What have you for Christmas?' we asked him. 'Nothing,' he said, 'Rover chased Daddy Christmas back up the chimney.' He had Rover with him on the lead. We tut-tutted, and gave Alec a play at our things. We were near his house, and his mother nodded at the door. He had nobody else.

Eddie Moore joined us. He, of course, had six-pence. He was stopping in our street from the country. His aunt, Mrs. Jackson, kept a wee shop. He stood still when he heard about Rover. 'What, that thing?' he laughed, 'that could chase nothing!' We set on him and gave him a roughing up. He ran up the street to Mrs. Jackson's and up the hall. Mrs. Jackson came out to see what was wrong, and Eddie Moore hid behind her skirt. 'What's all this?' she said. Eddie Moore got in first. 'All I said was imagine Rover chasing Daddy Christmas back up the chimney, and they nearly killed me,' he said.

Mrs. Jackson went inside, and came out with a bag of caramels. She gave them to Alec Reynolds. Then she bent down and lifted Rover and kissed him. Rover was only two weeks old. I think he was a mongrel. 'That Rover's a wild dog,' she said to Eddie Moore, 'he's trained to attack people coming down chimneys.'

The Eucharistic Congress

Whenever I was a kid in Belfast in the early 30's I was very fond of crossing the Border from time to time and visiting my fellow men who kicked with the left foot.

The Border in those days was the New Lodge Road. My purpose in making the odd safari into Comanche territory was, I must confess it, in order to shoot the line to an audience who didn't know I was doing it.

'Why are you skipping up and down like that?' a young lad standing at the corner of the New Lodge and North Queen Street asked me one day. He was about my own age — twelve. It wasn't surprising he should ask me. I had stopped in front of him and shadow boxed, touched my toes, and finally skipped, madly, using no rope, and snorting through my nose like a grampus.

'I'm training for the boxing', I told him.

'What's your name?' he asked me.

'Sam McAughtry', I said.

'Never heard of you', he remarked. The kids on his side of the fence knew their stuff on boxing. There were some nifty scrappers in the neighbourhood.

'No', says I, 'I'm sure you haven't heard of me. Not yet. But', I said, 'you've heard of my uncle, all right'.

'Who's your uncle?', he almost sneered.

'He's only Jack Doyle; that's all', I said, dancing all round him with the left glove a blur of movement. 'It's a long time since I've seen my Uncle Jack', I said, skipping away. 'I'd better go home and drop him a line, or he'll be complaining to my mother.'

I suppose you could say that was a fairly typical example of my trips across the frontier. On different occasions I was a schoolboy international goalkeeper, an American visitor named Zane Grey, or a lost little rich boy, looking for his father. It went something like this: 'You didn't happen to see my old man did you? He owns all these houses. He told me to inspect Trainfield Street to see if the houses are all right while he inspected Artillery Street. I wonder where he is, in the big car.'

But there was one time when I got my facts mixed up properly on the other side. I was walking along Lepper Street limping badly, looking for somebody to help me across the road so that I could explain how I got injured stopping a runaway horse and cart, when I spotted this table thing on the pavement, covered with linen, with flowers and silver things on it. 'What's that?' I asked this boy standing at a corner. He looked at me suspiciously. 'Do you not live here?' he asked me. 'How can I live here and in Australia at the same time?' I said sarcastically. 'It's the Eucharistic Congress', your man said.

I studied this thing very carefully, going past. Eucharistic Congress, eh? They were nice sounding words. Musical. Funny name, all the same. Eucharistic Congress. I made my way on down the New Lodge Road and along to the library. There was a new girl in charge of the children's books, so I tried the American accent on her. She dismissed me in a matter of minutes. I should have known not to try a name like Zane Grey on a librarian.

I took a slightly different road back along North Queen Street. And there, in front of the army barracks, was another one: table, flowers, linen and silver. I was about a hundred yards off it, when I heard somebody calling me. It was my mate Frankie Pattison. He lived in the street next to me. Frankie was fond of crossing the Border too, and sometimes I used to wonder whether he was related to Jack Doyle as well. 'What's that, do you think?' Frankie asked, as we approached the table. I looked at him in astonishment. 'Do you mean to tell me you don't know what that is'? I said. He shook his head, studying it as we walked past. It certainly looked very nice. 'That', I said patiently, 'is a Eucharistic Congress. Imagine not knowing that'. I shook my head, unable to take such ignorance in.

'What's that? he wanted to know. 'It's beyond your understanding', I said, and turned up Hardinge Street before I was caught on.

The young fellow who'd first told me about it was still standing in Lepper Street. 'D'ye see that Eucharistic Congress', I said. He nodded. 'What is it?' I asked him point blank. 'All I know about it', he said, 'is that it comes round every hundred years'. I thanked him and limped away, thoughtfully.

That night I turned up at our street corner. The boys were all there. We talked about this and that. 'I was over by the New Lodge today', I said, 'and I met a very interesting fellow. He had a very bad limp. He got it stopping a runaway horse and cart. They had to take the bone right out', I explained, 'and now the leg's all flabby, like rubber'. The lads all shook their heads in sympathy.

'What was the name of that table and flowers again?' Frankie Pattison asked, 'I was telling the lads here that you know all about it'.

'There's these two tables, covered in linen and flowers and real silver', I said, 'they're called Eucharistic Congresses. They only bring them out every hundred years'.

'All the same', Frankie said, 'they must have been well looked after since eighteen and thirty two'. All the lads nodded.

"Eucharistic Congresses are all like that', I said knowledgeably, 'they're made specially to last. The man that looks after them's a brother of Jack Doyle, the boxer.'

The Old Alma Mater

Every time I see one of those memory lane pieces in the paper by a man of education I tense myself for the bit about the fine, sensitive classics master, and his lasting influence on the writer. The gentle Latin scholar, who has taught the writer to face up to life honestly, and never to take the easy way out.

I know perfectly well that people are going to regard me as a second-rate cad for my cynical reception of this sort of thing. I know I have never been next nor near a good school, or even a below-average one, but the way I see it's this: if a newspaper's prepared to publish your reminiscences then you're somebody important. And nobody I know ever got to be important by facing up to life honestly, and never taking the easy way out.

I'll bet you an even fiver that the only people who have ever managed to get by on that advice are the classics masters themselves.

And I'll tell you this much: if Mister Chips is going to speak to me down the corridors of time, he'd better be telling me how to make a fast buck, or else I'm switched off — over and out.

In the school I went to, in North Belfast, in the 1930's, we didn't have such a thing as a sensitive master. If you did what you were told you weren't hit. That was the limit of their sensitivity.

There was one time, all the same, when I thought

we'd got a gentle and noble master to set us all an example. His name was Gordon, and he was a temporary replacement for old Tipping, who broke his wrist when he hit the wall instead of John Murphy. It happened during grammar, when we were parsing and analysing. Old Tipping overheard John Murphy say to Tommy Walsh: 'What's parsing about?' and he misunderstood it, so he swung a violent blow at him, and, as I say, he hit the wall.

'Listen boys and girls,' this new man Gordon said, 'I don't believe in the cane. You are all on your honour to tell the truth instead.'

Well, I immediately tickled big May Morton under the oxter. She let out a wild scream. I stood up: 'I openly admit tickling big May Morton under the oxter,' I said, loudly. Artie Hughes stood up next: 'While your man was tickling big May,' he said, 'I knocked off two Woodbines out of his schoolbag, and I don't mind owning up to it.' Next thing I let Artie have one on the whiskers: 'I confess to thumping Artie Hughes on the gub,' I announced.

Like lightning Mister Gordon had me pinned to the wall by the thrapple: 'If you don't stop acting the lig I'll hammer you into the ground like a nail,' he snarled. Then he flung me into my seat, half stunned. 'It's just caning I don't believe in,' he told the class, 'outside of that you can have it whatever way you want.'

Mister Gordon went back to the blackboard. 'Always remember this,' he told us, 'just because you don't know the form of a horse doesn't mean it can't run.'

I knew what he meant, from the bruises on my thrapple. I never forgot that piece of advice. If I

ever get to be important I must write to the
papers about it. . .

Galloper Thompson's Ghost

If you go down Cosgrave Street in Tiger's Bay, Belfast, and stop at the spot where Lilliput Street makes a junction you'd be in a brave desolate stretch of tundra today. The right hand side of Cosgrave Street has been nibbled and hoked away, and only the rats live now on the ground where four generations of lovely people were born, and played, and lived out their lives.

Lilliput Street took its name from a country house in the area once occupied by a well-known family named Thomson, and when I was a boy in the district fifty years ago the name Thomson had a special meaning.

But if you were at the corner of Lilliput Street today one thing you would notice amongst the surrounding decay would be the cracked concrete road at the point where it joins Cosgrave Street. And nobody would blame you for thinking that this was just part of the senility and wrinkles and bald spots that can be seen in the whole of the inner city. But no. We did that, our crowd in Tiger's Bay, one Eleventh of July — 1930, to be precise. We did it with the biggest bonfire North Belfast had ever seen. We cracked the concrete, and heated the walls of half a dozen houses till the families in them had to evacuate for two hours. They came from the streets around in their hundreds to see our bonfire. When it was at its height the police came to see it, too, out of curiosity, wondering how we got the half of the stuff we were burning, but they never found out, thank goodness.

It all started when we were standing at the street corner talking about Galloper Thomson's ghost, that Eleventh Night. We were at the same time feeling rather inadequate because of our small bonfire. It was a real miserable looking thing, compared to the one at the corner of Mervue Street. It was Dan McDonough who connected the two things, in a brilliant piece of tactical thinking.

'There's a huge pile of old scrap timber up in the brickworks,' he said, 'if we could only get it down here we'd have a bonfire that would make Mervue Street's look like a box of matches.'

'But that timber's too heavy to carry down here,' we protested. 'Right,' says Dan McDonough, 'so we pinch Porterbelly McClean's horse and cart.' 'But we'll be spotted by old Aggie Scanlon,' we said. Aggie was Porterbelly's cousin. She was also less than fond of rowdy young fellows, like us. Her house was beside the stables.

Dan had this one thought out. 'If we wait till dark,' he said, winking, 'Aggie'll think it's Galloper Thomson's ghost, when she hears the horse.'

It was a brilliant plan. Aggie Scanlon had Galloper Thomson's ghost on the brain. She kept telling the whole neighbourhood at least once a week how she'd heard the sound of the horse in the darkness, and how, terrified, she'd looked out of the window, and seen the cloaked figure, mounted on his fierce steed, riding up Cosgrave Street, towards McBrien's the greengrocers. 'Did his horse stop for a turnip when it reached McBrien's?'

Willie Forsythe asked her one day, but she ignored the mockery. Galloper, we suspected, was more than a ghost to Aggie. She was an old maid; I think she was sort of half hoping the horseman would carry her off some night.

That Eleventh Night we waited till it was dark, then we climbed into Porterbelly's yard and slid the bar to open the gate. Dan McDonough worked for a carter at the docks, so he knew about Clydesdales. We manoeuvred Porterbelly's horse into the heavy coal cart, then we led it down the entry and out into the street. The neighbours spotted us at once: all except Aggie Scanlon, there was no sign of life from her house. 'Watch yourself,' the neighbours warned, 'Fairy Feet the peeler's about.' So we got offside right away, made our way to the brickworks on the Limestone Road, with about fifteen of us up on the cart. Then we loaded her up as much as she would take with the big baulks of timber, and drove her back to Lilliput Street.

Well I'm telling you — talk about a bonfire. You could have seen it from Carrickfergus. The lads from Mervue Street were knocked sick. The bricks of the very houses were nearly red hot, but we gave the families a bit of a hand to cool the walls down with buckets of water, till the fire went down a bit. Fairy Feet and one of his mates came up, with their night hats and sticks: 'Where did you get that wood?' they wanted to know. 'We carried it down from the brickworks,' we told them. 'Hm', Fairy Feet said, 'you must have been eating some very special porridge, to manage that lot.' Then he saw the buckets of water being dashed against the walls. 'Right,' he said, 'I'll lift one or two of you for endangering them houses.' 'What are you talking about,' Alec Kenny said: he lived in the one that was getting the biggest roasting, 'that house is so damp that it would take a bonfire twice the size to dry it out.' So there was no more from the cops. And there was no more from the lads of Mervue Street. And that bonfire stayed in till halfway through the Twelfth Day.

Next morning Dan McDonough asked Aggie Scanlon if she'd heard Galloper Thomson's ghost. 'If that ghost had any sense,' she said, 'it stayed at home last night.' 'Why?' Dan asked her. 'Because if it had come out,' she said, 'it was running the risk of getting knocked down by you idiots, pinching Porterbelly's Clydesdale and cart.'

Private Enterprise

Somebody said the other day that the supermarkets were going to put the small neighbourhood shops out of existence. All I can say to that
is that they wouldn't have put the small neighbourhood shops that used to operate in the 1920's and
'30's out of existence. Quite the reverse.

What that supermarket argument rests on is the
fact that goods are sold with only a bare margin
of profit. Well so what? Sure that's nothing. All
along York Street in Belfast shops of every des-
cription sold every conceivable product at the bare
margin of profit when I was a kid. There was a
thirty yard stretch of North Queen Street where
three grocers operated on one side of the road,
and a fourth one sat on the other side. And the
whole four of them got a living out of it, even
though they were cutting the tar out of each
other. I ought to know. I was a message boy in one
of them.

Actually my boss, and the man who owned the
grocer's beside him used to work for the same
man at one time. When this man died he left the
shop to my boss, and the other fellow was so
annoyed at being left out of things that he opened
up his shop in opposition, and started to steal his
customers by getting in below his prices.

Right, I can hear somebody saying, that's just
the way the supermarkets carry on. Undercut,

and bingo goes the rival shop. But no. What happened in those days, in fact, was that shopkeepers didn't stand behind their counters waiting for customers to discover them. No, they sent their message boys to people's houses to ask if they wanted, say, ham, for it was the cheapest on the road. And the message boy stood at the door and took the customer's order, and he went back to the shop and wrapped it up, and then he carried it to the customer's house again. It would take a brave good supermarket to stand up in the face of that. The customer might have started off with just a quarter of ham at practically cost price, but gradually she would have been coaxed into buying more and more goods.

Christmas was when the grocers really wooed the customers. Two days before it, my boss would have sent Davy McFall the van driver and me to Ballynahinch to buy eggs and chickens. We left at about six in the morning, the pony trotting along the country road at a nice easy clip, and me sitting up there alongside Davy drinking in the good fresh air, and asking him stupid questions, like why did farmers persist in growing parsnips when so many wee boys hated them.

We would take about twelve dozen of live chickens on board, and the full of the van of eggs, and by the time we got back to North Queen Street it would be six o'clock in the evening. We would get a mug of tea and some bread and cheese and then it was upstairs and into the killing of the chickens, and plucking them.

The next night, Christmas Eve, it was the tradition that the message boy delivered a chicken to each good customer, and a dozen eggs to the poorer ones. This was a time of great excitement, for the customer handed over the Christmas box, when she got her present from the shop. All the message boys on the road told manifest lies to each other about the amount they got for tips, but I suppose it would have averaged out at about a pound, which was enough nearly to turn a boy's head in those days. However, once they got home the problem was eased, because their mothers were only too glad to relieve them of the responsibility of spending it.

Practically every shop on the road at that time organised raffles and competitions, the prize sat prominently in the window, and it looked very inviting indeed, especially to a woman with a big family. 'A free ticket with every half crown's worth of goods' the notice would say, and as a result the people would spread their custom right along the road so that they would have an interest in as many raffles as possible.

The wage for a message boy in my time was four or five shillings. For that you worked a fifty three hour week. If news ever reached the street corner that a message boy's job was going in a particular shop there was a mad sprint by every boy present to try to get there first. The job had its perks over and above the five bob, of course, for it would be a very stupid message boy indeed who couldn't accidentally knock a chocolate biscuit to the floor as he happened to walk past it. Indeed there was a sort of organised business about it in my time, for a group of message boys used to meet down the Shore Road every morning, when we were out taking our morning orders, and a whole barter system operated within the group. You could have got, for example, two Woodbines for an apple and an orange. I remember one time getting a coconut for a pocketful of sugar lumps. You would wonder that our bosses could have carried our barter business as well as fight off the opposition from other shops.

But they did. And that's why the supermarkets wouldn't have counted in those days. They wouldn't have lasted a month. For goodness sake those four grocers in North Queen Street alone would have sorted out Tesco before their breakfast.

The Fokker Tripe

The Fokker Tripe appeared in the window of Chapman's shop in Tiger's Bay, on Christmas Eve, 1931. It hung from the ceiling on a thread that was almost invisible, so that it seemed to be hovering in the air, alive in every brace and strut.

It was a German Triplane, with a big, black cross behind the cockpit. The model was lovingly made from balsa wood and doped linen; it was silvery-blue, and the round nose was bright red. When the boy saw it he stopped stone dead, and stared, and stared. For this was a replica of the Fokker Triplane flown by the legendary Werner Voss, ace of aces.

The boy was so hypnotised that he forgot to hurry past Chapman's shop with his head down, as he had intended, for, only the day before, he had knocked off yet another Great War flying magazine. Waiting until the shop was empty, and the widow's head was bent over her knitting, he had crouched below counter level, tiptoed into the shop, shoved the flying book up his jersey, and glided out again, like Groucho Marx. For the couple of days after KO'ing a book he always rushed past, head turned, in case Mrs. Chapman had nailed him.

He was a seaman's son: 'God bless my daddy and send him safe home,' he said every night, on his knees, 'and God bless my mother, and all my brothers and sisters, and Tiny the dog'. Then he would frown, and add: 'God, please excuse me for KO'ing the books, and help me to sneaky them out of the coalhole, for if my mother sees them she'll put me in a home. For ever and ever, amen.'

He went into the shop: 'How much is the aeroplane?' he asked. The widow looked at him out of her watery eyes: 'You're a good boy,' she said, 'I see you in the church choir. Tell me who it is steals the flying books every month?' 'It might be Alec McDermott,' he said. There was no such boy. 'You tell Alec McDermott from me that I'm on his track,' Mrs. Chapman said severely. 'How much for the aeroplane?' he asked again. 'Eight and six,' she said. Dejected, he went outside, to study its every lovely line hungrily.

This was the famous Tripe, scourge of the Allies in 1917. In the first three weeks that he had flown it Werner Voss shot down twenty two British aircraft. He was a better pilot than Goering, or Udet, and as good as Richthofen. It took Mc Cudden and six other British aces to bring him down.

The boy's mother had told him to bring his chorister's surplice home to be washed. He went into St. Barnabas' church near the New Lodge Road, opened the locker in the robing room, and took his surplice out. Then he sat in a pew. The chancel arch rose over his head. On it were the words: 'Seek Ye The Lord Where He May Be Found.' The boy put his hands before his face: 'No matter which way I look at this, Lord,' he said, 'it always ends up with me put in a home. Am I right?' God pursed his lips: 'You certainly picked a lovely time, didn't you?' He said. The boy nodded: 'I know,' he said, 'Christmas.' 'Exactly,'

God replied, 'eleven books knocked off. That's Mrs. Chapman's Christmas box. And now you're going daft to get that Fokker Tripe.'

The boy slipped to his knees, and prayed: 'Almighty and most merciful Father, we have erred and strayed from thy ways like lost sheep; we have followed too much the devices and desires of our own hearts, and there is no health in us.' 'No,' said God, 'there's not.'

The boy rose, put the surplice below his arm, and left the church. As he went through the door his brain started to work. . .

There was nobody in the house when he got back. This was a miracle. Ten people lived here, in a two-up, two-down. He had never seen it empty before. He carried the eleven magazines out of the coalhole and took them up the narrow street to Chapman's shop. It was empty. He could see the top of her head, bowed over her knitting. He crept in carefully, spread the flying books all across the shelf, and tiptoed out again. Ten minutes later he went in again: 'I told that Alec McDermott what you said,' he announced. The widow was nearly out of breath: 'I never saw the like of it,' she said, 'flying books everywhere.'

'Do you need a message boy?' he asked. 'Do you know, that's like the answer to a prayer', she said, 'I've nobody to give my customers their Christmas presents. Would you like to do it?' 'I'll do it for the aeroplane,' he said, and she agreed.

The boy worked till ten that night, going round the customers and giving them their Christmas presents from the shop — a box of chocolates each. He collected ten shillings for himself, from the customers, and he left eight and threepence into the cash drawer when the widow wasn't looking, being eleven times ninepence, for the loss of the magazine sales. Then he took the Fokker Tripe in his hands, as though he was holding the venerated ashes of Werner Voss.

Voss was shot down on a grey morning, late in 1917. It took ten minutes for McCudden's flight to execute the handsome, shy airman. As they circled and circled, he rolled and spun and stalled through the spitting bullets. But Rhys Davids got him in the end. When the squadron celebrated that afternoon, both McCudden and Rhys Davids waved the drinks away: 'It's a pity he had to die,' they said.

'Your wee aeroplane's just lovely,' his mother said, when he got home.

'Here's a box of chocolates for Christmas,' he said. She gave him a kiss. 'And I've got a present for you,' she told him. He found out what it was next morning. It was all the flying books that he'd taken out of the coalhole. 'Mrs. Chapman let me have them cheap,' his mother said. The boy raised his eyes to heaven, helplessly.

'I hope that fixes everything up, God,' he said on his knees on Christmas night. 'Lord now lettest Thou thy servant depart in peace, according to thy word.'

'That's the wrong prayer,' the Lord told him, 'but it'll do in the circumstances.'

Real Hundred Per Cent Food

Tell me this: why is it you never read articles in the papers about real hundred per cent food? Why do editors think that all we ever eat is fish souffle, or salmon and cucumber mousse, or orange duck casserole?

There's hundreds of thousands of people in this country wouldn't thank you for that stuff. You take a Belfast shipyard man who's been subjected all day to a cutting wind coming straight across the Irish Sea, and him with four pints and two or three half 'uns of whiskey in him after he finishes work. When a man like that walks over the door looking for a tightener what would you give for your chances if you offered him, say, shrimp and cheese flan? You'd get a dig in the gub, that's what you would get.

What that man needs is what you get when you take and drop a pig's knee into water, add onions and carrots and any amount of peas, and boil it till a spoon'll stand in it without falling over. That's the sort of grub that these cookery editors want to think about. The sort of grub that puts him to sleep beside the fire where he can't do any damage, like buying drink out of turn. The women of long ago discovered that wee rule for a happy home. You wouldn't have found them feeding their men like a bird and making him that chirpy that he wants to hop out, looking for another bird.

And by the way, I would like to see a newspaper campaign aimed at finding out what has happened to buttermilk. You never see buttermilk mentioned by the cookery experts. I'm talking about the sort of buttermilk that we used to get out of the grocer's for tuppence a quart, before the war. Where on earth has it gone? They're making butter, aren't they? Well then they're making buttermilk. Are they throwing it all away or something? I know one thing for sure. That stuff sold in bottles that they call buttermilk is nothing of the sort. It tastes like water out of car batteries.

When you were sent for buttermilk long ago you took a can with you, and when you were going for sweet milk it was a jug you took. It was all right to have a swig out of the buttermilk on the way home, but it wasn't all right to drink the sweet milk. Willie Fawcett's mother used to make him spit out on the street to see if he'd been drinking the sweet milk. There's an interesting story about Willie Fawcett in connection with buttermilk too. After showing him the effect of centrifugal force when you whirl a quart of buttermilk round and round I told Willie once that two whirls round made the buttermilk stick to the bottom, and if you held it upside down over your head nothing would happen. He was covered in buttermilk from top to toe but he hit me across the side of the head with the empty can so I don't know who came out of it the worst. But anyway it was buttermilk and spuds that put the lining into many a stomach before any of these fancy dishes were heard of.

What about tripe? You never see anything in

the papers about tripe, do you? Not fashionable enough, you see. You can't start in about the appropriate wine, and about whether you'll start off with asparagus when it's tripe you're talking about, sure you can't? And yet tripe's a very satisfactory dish. Whenever my mother brought tripe into the house long years ago, she had to get it into the saucepan and light the gas tout' suite otherwise there was wholesale pilfering of it while it was still raw. With plenty of salt it was hard to whack.

Actually tripe has a certain calming effect on people. I don't know if you're aware of that, but I have seen it proved. There used to be a public house in Tiger's Bay and the proprietor of that place knew exactly what the power of tripe was. There was a sing song in this bar, you see, and there's no need for me to go into detail about what that means. Wherever you get a sing song you get fights, don't you? 'The best of order for the singer', the self-appointed chairman says, but there's always a couple of customers who didn't come in to listen to singers. They came in for a yarn over their drink, and there's no chairman going to make them shut up.

This proprietor had a sixth sense for flashpoint situations like that, and just as the chairman was about to vacate the chair and fracture a couple of jaws in came the barman with saucers of raw tripe all round. Sprinkled with vinegar and any amount of salt on it. I'm telling you, by the time the customers got that down them their good natures had all come back to them again.

You never read about things like that in the quality press, sure you don't?

Not mind you that I don't wax lyrical sometimes

about the finer lines in food myself the way these sophisticated writers do. Do you know that juice that you get with pineapple chunks? That's what I like. I remember saying to Willie Forsythe one time when I was a kid, 'D'ye see that juice that comes with pineapple chunks?' 'Yes', he said. 'Well', says I, 'do ye know what I would love to do?' 'No', he says. 'I would love', says I, 'to dive into a swimming bath full of it.'

Of course Willie Forsythe had to go one better. 'I would love to dive into a swimming bath full of ice cream', he said.

Imagine diving into a swimming bath full of ice cream.

Stupid ass!

The Sunday Parade

'How do they do it?' Alec Walsh asked, for the umpteenth time.

The two of us were standing on the Antrim Road near Fortwilliam, on a summer Sunday evening in the year of our Lord 1937. We were sixteen. Sixteen, and we couldn't get a dog to bark at us.

Almost as far as the eye could see the Antrim Road seemed to be black with sixteen-year-old fellows linking girls that they'd picked up on the Sunday Parade. We could see the process going on all round us. Two dolls would come along letting on not to look to right or left, but actually missing nothing. Before they would reach our length a couple of fellows like ourselves standing at the wall would call something like: 'Does your Ma know yer out?' or else: 'Would you go for a loaf?' or maybe: 'Hey you — you've a quare leg for button boots.'

The girls would giggle, slow up, if they fancied the boys: then the fellows would be over to them like greased lightning and there you were, another two pairs dandering towards the sort of experience that Alec Walsh and me were nearly going daft to sample.

'What's the matter with us?' Alec Walsh would say, looking at me suspiciously. Right enough, I would say to myself, he didn't pick much of an enticement when he took me along to the Sunday Parade. I was like a beanpole. I wore my big brother's shirts, and you could see the stitching up the back of the collar where they'd been turned in. My suit had been handed down to such an extent that by the time I was finished with it Oliver Twist wouldn't have accepted it.

'Don't blame me,' I said to Alec Walsh on the weary way home, 'I'm doing the best I can.' Just with that two numbers came sallymandering along towards us. They had mill doffer written all over them — bold and pretty, and weighing up the sales talk they were getting from the boys lined along the pavement. One of them was especially striking: she had that blue-dark hair, and kiss curls all along her brow. Just to show Alec Walsh that I had a contribution to make I found myself shouting at her: 'Hey — are your curls stuck on with condensed milk?'

The wee girl stopped, outraged. 'I say you,' she said, 'you watch yourself or you'll get this high heel in your gub.' Inside me — a long way inside me — something was telling me that this skirt was a smasher, but ninety-nine per cent of me was standing, wilting under her gaze, wanting to dissolve into steam, vanish in a puff, and never run the risk of being looked at like that again.

The two girls went on and Alec Walsh looked at me with open disgust. 'Come on and we'll go down to Thompson's shop,' he said.

I would have paid him compensation if I'd had any money. It wasn't Alec's fault we couldn't get anything in the line of a doll. He was good looking, with good broad shoulders, wavy hair and a nose a wee bit like Jack Doyle the boxer. No, it was me. I was abnormally skinny. In our

111

house they called me a relic of the Indian famine.

Standing in Thompson's shop, drinking his half of a tuppenny bottle of grape fruit, Alec Walsh came to a sudden decision: 'To hell with it,' he said, 'I'm getting a black shirt with pearl buttons down the collar. I don't care if you get one or not,' he went on, defiantly, 'it's the only way we're going to get a bit of stuff.'

I looked at him thunderstruck. A black shirt? With pearly buttons? For goodness sake Alec Walsh and I had been sneering for weeks at fellows who wore them. It had started when George Raft wore one in a gangster picture: like magic they had appeared all along York Street and Tiger's Bay: on sixteen year olds, with short haircuts and their hair smothered in brilliantine and parted in the middle.

Standing at the foot of Cosgrave Street on many an evening Alec Walsh and I had marvelled at the dozens of them, all looking like George Raft, and walking with George Raft's shoulder-swinging dancer's walk. All with their double-breasted jackets flapping on the swivel button. We called them the York Street Fusiliers, with their uniforms and all their orders.

Alec Walsh went out of Thompson's shop without saying any more. 'See you,' I shouted after him, but he didn't take any notice.

He wasn't at the corner on any of the nights during the week. 'I saw Alec Walsh with Tommy Waugh last night,' somebody told me. Oh well, says I, that's that. He'll not half pick up the skirt now, all right. Tommy Waugh not only wore the black shirt, he had a double breasted waistcoat as well. There was no possibility of failure when you went out with that sort of a rig.

112

The next Sunday evening I was standing at Fortwilliam. I was with Jack Surgenor. It was all I could manage. When I had called for Alec Walsh his sister had told me that he'd gone out with Tommy Waugh.

Jack Surgenor was brainy. He was cracked about wirelesses. Up there on the Antrim Road, in the middle of the Sunday Parade he was talking about electrons. After a while I got so disheartened that I got a tennis ball out of my pocket, put a threepenny bit down at the foot of the wall, and started bouncing the ball against the wall, trying to hit the coin. Jack Surgenor was telling me about the Heaviside Layer.

Suddenly a girl's voice stopped me dead. 'Hello cheeky face.'

I caught the ball and turned round. It was the girl with the kiss curls and her mate. They were smiling. They were standing beside us. Impulsively I said, before I had time to be embarrassed: 'I'm sorry for saying that to you last week.' 'And so you should be,' she said, still smiling, so help me God.

Jack Surgenor had stopped talking about electrons. He pointed to me, perfectly poised: 'Did he actually criticise you?' he asked Kiss Curls. She nodded, her eyes dancing. Jack Surgenor extended his arm, 'allow me,' he said, 'to make amends.'

I was watching this, totally turned to jelly. I was even worse when the girl turned to me and said: 'No, I want to link blushy face here,' and with that she took a hold of my arm and there we were, part of the Sunday Parade for the first time in history.

A hundred yards further on a voice calls: 'You've a quare leg for button boots,' then he sees me and

nearly collapses. It was Alec Walsh in his George
Raft shirt. 'Knock it off, Walsh,' I says to him,
'that's my woman you're talking about.'

Bernadette

When I was sixteen, in 1937, I used to work in a wholesale clothing warehouse. It was located in Howard Street, in the centre of Belfast, just over a mile from our house in Hillman Street. I walked the journey four times a day. For over a year the only walking that I enjoyed was the final journey home at the end of the day, for I detested that job to the soles of my feet.

It took exactly twenty minutes, walking briskly. Down Hillman Street and turn right into North Queen Street. Here, after only a few yards, I was in Catholic country. Here the newspaper placards changed from the Northern Whig and the News Letter to the Irish News. The long wall of Victoria army barracks ran along my right hand side, its embrasures conjuring up in my mind exciting visions of beseiged Foreign Legionnaires, and burnoused arabs, charging, perhaps, up Henry Street, in the shadow of the flax spinning mill.

To while away the time I used to whistle bag-pipe tunes to myself, for I was a piper in Castleton Temperance Pipe Band: 'Established 1900' it said on Castleton's drum. 'The Burning Sands of Egypt,' would take me from home to the New Lodge Road. Then, passing the long, white-painted barrack wall, and its Spanish Civil War slogans, I would strike up another four-part march, the Seventy-Ninth's Farewell to Gibraltar. This would take me across Clifton Street, and, entering Carrick Hill, I would go into a tricky six-part piece called The Highland Wedding full of difficult grips and grace notes. The last part of the journey towards purgatory would be accomplished to the air of The Flowers of the Forest — a sad dirge completely in keeping with my mood.

Sometimes, instead of pretending that I was piping, I would play the part of the drum major, a splendid figure, with high busby, tight chin strap, and majestic carriage. I could just see myself holding the silver mace in my left hand, and swinging the right arm up to the level of my shoulder. And one summer's day, on my way back to work after lunch, I was completely lost in this dream, leading Castleton triumphantly back to Tiger's Bay, after beating the Fintan Lalor band in the Irish piping final down in Dublin. My mother was there in the crowd, pointing me out to her neighbours; folks had come from miles around to see the famous McAughtry, world champion drum major: the roar of the crowd was deafening. . . .

'They're all laughing at you, hey.'

With a heart-stepping jolt I came back to North Queen Street. A girl had caught up with me, had tapped me on the shoulder. She was smiling, and pointing. Over at the corner of the New Lodge Road a group of left-footers of my own age were busting themselves laughing.

I nearly fainted. I went redder than a pillar box, then I turned pale. As I hurried away along the side of the barrack wall I felt as though I wanted to vanish, never to return.

'You looked awful funny, so you did.' Oh God, the girl was still with me, at my shoulder. I was almost in tears. I couldn't look at her. It would have

116

to be a girl, wouldn't it? If it had only been a boy I could have opened up with a short jab to the gub; a speedy conclusion would have been reached, one way or the other. But a girl? I had never, in my life, made casual conversation with a girl. When the girls round our way tried to get me into the nightly boy-girl slagging match that went on at the corner, I used to pretend to be angry, and clear off. I put a few inches on to my step to get away from this one, but she was still with me, as we neared St. Patrick's chapel.

Passing it, she crossed herself. The lot. The full works. Crossed herself head and shoulders. Not even the quick scrape with the thumb on the brow that the boys of the neighbourhood went in for. That's all it took now. To be seen with one of the other side. There surely couldn't be any more to this disaster.

'What's your name?' As we entered Carrick Hill I looked at her for the first time. I didn't know her brown eyes, her smiling mouth, her wide brow. She came to my shoulder, and I could look down on her shining dark hair. She wore a jacket that had seen better days, but so did everybody. Her face was turned up to me, and I noted the snub nose, the white teeth, the lower lip turned in just a little. 'What's your name?' she asked again. She stopped. 'I go up here,' she said, pointing to the Old Lodge Road.

'Sam,' I said, 'they call me Sam.' She crinkled her eyes: 'Nearly everybody's called Sam, where you live,' she said. Then we both laughed together. 'Well, I know *your* name, at least,' I told her. 'What is it, then?' she asked, coming closer. 'It's Teresa,' I said, 'everybody round your way's called Teresa.'

She hit me playfully on the arm. 'Everybody's

not,' she said. 'What *is* your name?' I asked. Suddenly I wanted to know. 'It's Bernadette,' she said, and turned away, 'maybe you'll know me better now,' she called, and I stood still, watching her go.

Yes, I said, as I made my way to work, I'll know you again. Bernadette.

And always, after, I looked for her on the road. I never played the pipe tunes for looking. But I never saw Bernadette again.

So she never knew. Bernadette never knew that I loved her.

Return to Hillman Street

When I was fourteen years of age our family moved from Cosgrave Street in Tiger's Bay to another part of North Belfast, Hillman Street, beside the New Lodge Road.

The distance involved in the move wasn't any more than a couple of hundred yards or so, in a straight line, but in terms of progress on the social scale it was a vertical take-off of a good half mile. For one thing, the Hillman Street house had a parlour, and for another, it had front and back attics. And as if that wasn't heady enough, the back attic had been converted into a bathroom.

Mind you, the bath was fitted with only a single cold water tap. We had the reason explained to us by Albert Lutton, a plumber, who lived in the next street. 'I want you to fit the hot water into that bathroom,' my mother said to him. 'I'll put it in for you, Lizzie,' he said, 'the only thing is, you'll have to keep well clear of the bathroom when the geyser's turned on.' 'Why is that then?' my mother asked him. 'Because,' says he, 'it'll blow the back attic into the next street. That's why. It's all to do with the pressure you see.' So any time we wanted a bath we had to hump buckets of hot water up the stairs the full height of the house, but we didn't mind in the slightest. It was better than the Cosgrave Street way — pulling the curtain across the scullery, getting on with the operation, only to break off, cursing and blinding, when some of the family, just in from the street, barged through the scullery on the way out to the yard, and caught you out with nothing on but the soapsuds.

When my father came home from the sea on his next trip he was quietly pleased with my mother for making the move. 'This is more the sort of place where a ship's donkeyman ought to live,' he said, 'it's a house where you can really entertain your friends.' And the very first night he was home he invited about eight men round from Jimmy McGrane's pub, instead of the usual five. They all sat in the parlour agreeing that the move had to come sooner or later: 'You'll not know yourself, with the parlour and all,' they told my mother. 'Not only that,' says she, beaming, 'but the previous woman left her pulley lines still up on the kitchen ceiling: talk about acting the lady!'

Mind you, the rent was no joke: eight shillings a week, compared to four and six for the Cosgrave Street house. But it was money well spent. I slept in the front room with our Jim and Tommy; my mother had the back room to herself for a change, and Charlotte slept in the front attic. We hardly ever used the parlour, of course, but in no time at all we had a bit of nice furniture in there — a three-piece suite and a china cabinet and a square of inlaid lino on the floor.

It was a great feeling, living round in Hillman Street. I suppose it was actually the first sign of improvement in our fortunes. The neighbours weren't as close to us as the people of Tiger's Bay had been, of course, but they made us welcome for all that. One of the first things that happened to me there was an invitation to help to put up the streamers for the Twelfth of July. With a couple of other lads of the district I hammered nails into the walls and then tied the streamers to the nails. This meant climbing up the ladder — the first time I had ever climbed one with full permission. When we'd finished that the local Unionist Association gave us half a crown each: a very nice introduction to the new neighbourhood.

My mother joined the Mothers' Union soon after we went to live in Hillman Street. She used to come back from the meetings and tell us all about the addresses that the Bishop's wife, and the rector's wife had given. And she used to go to the bus runs and bring back sticks of rock from places like Garron Tower and Bushmills. We didn't know if they were north south east or west of us, but we would sit and listen to all the details of the places from mother.

There was a moneylender along Lepper Street nearby who did a steady trade with the people of Hillman Street. Her name was Jinny Ward. She was a Catholic, and she lived in Catholic territory. I had the job of carrying mother's instalments over to her on a Friday night and one night a couple of local lads started to act the idiot with me just before I got to Jinny Ward's house. 'Say your prayers,' one of them said: 'Our Father who art in heaven,' I said. We were all wise to that one. If we'd said: 'Our Father which art in heaven' we were in severe trouble. But just with that Jinny Ward came to the door. 'What are you saying that for?' she wanted to know. 'Because,' I said. I didn't want to bring anybody else into a private matter. Well, Jinny Ward let fly with a right uppercut across the gub of one of these young lads. 'You let him alone,' she shouted, and the pair of them took off like Mick the Miller, no doubt saying their own prayers in earnest, for Jinny Ward carried a lot of influence in the neighbourhood.

Nowadays the wee boys round that district don't need to ask the same question. They're all Catholics together, although mind you, it's a moot point as to whether their mothers are as pleased to be there as mine was.

Up above the doors are the nails that we hammered in forty-five years ago to hold the streamers. I pointed them out to a skinny fourteen-year-old: 'D'ye know what those nails are for?' I asked him. He shook his head. 'They're for holding streamers,' I told him. He looked again: 'You would need a ladder,' he said.

'If you ever want to put streamers up there,' I said, 'I'll buy you a ladder.'

When Uncle James Slowed Up

Before the war my Uncle James went to work in London as a labourer. It was in 1934. Afterwards he settled down to being a bus conductor in Belfast, but that year he worked in London gave my Uncle James a good few stories that he told for years afterwards, and mind you he was a great story teller, the same man.

My favourite story was the one about the first job he got. He was down a trench with the spade, doing the foundations for a big new building.

He was small, my Uncle James, and wiry: a very active man. He'd been out of work for a good many months and he couldn't have been more skinned — indeed he had been hard enough pushed to raise the boat money over — so he wanted to create a good impression. Away he went at the digging a mile a minute throwing the earth up and over his head and on to the surface as if it was coming out of a hosepipe or something. 'Take it easy', this old Welsh navvy beside him said, after watching him in fascination for about half an hour. He reached out a hand and stopped my Uncle James's frantic progress. 'Always remember', the old fellow said, 'that when you start digging you should start at the speed you intend to finish at'.

Now no matter how you look at it that statement sounds very profound. My Uncle James was very much impressed. 'Right enough', he says to this Welshman, 'you've got a point there', so he leans on his spade, considers the profundity of the thing for a minute or two, and starts back into the digging at three quarters of his original speed.

Five cubic yards later the Welshman reaches over and stops him again, shaking his head. 'The speed you're going to finish at', he says, 'remember?' 'Right y'are', says my Uncle James, and slows down to half the rate. 'Paddy', says the Welshman, 'how long are you at the game?' 'This is the first time I've actually done any digging', my Uncle James tells him. 'I thought that', the Welshman says, 'have you no regard at all for your workmates?' 'Why, what do you mean?' my Uncle James asks him. 'Because', the Welshman says, 'if that's the speed that you intend to finish at the foreman's going to expect the rest of us to do the same. In fact', the old fellow told him, "if you're the instigation of us having to go at that rate don't be one bit surprised if you get the whole lot of us sacked'.

Now if my Uncle James was anything he was a compassionate man. He had run the streets long enough himself to appreciate his workmates' anxiety. He looked up and down the foundation trench. Sure enough the squad of about six navvies all nodded their heads seriously, leaning on their spades. And now that my Uncle James came to be studying the rest of the work force he noticed right enough that he had shifted more English earth in the short time he'd been working that morning than the whole lot of them put together.

That was absolutely in character for my Uncle James of course. He was quick and effective in everything he did and he never was anything else. Just to show you what I mean I might as well tell you about the night he sent a mate of his down from the grandstand at Celtic Park in Belfast with a fiver to back a dog for him. This fellow ran down the steps of the stand with the fiver in his hand heading for the bookies on the rails. But at the foot of the grandstand he carried out a severe alteration of course to starboard and headed for the nearest exit.

Now for those people who like arithmetic the distance between my Uncle James's traitorous friend and the exit was fifty yards, and the distance from where my Uncle James was standing watching the performance was a further fifteen yards. Yet when your man drew abreast of the gate he found my Uncle James standing with a hurt look on his face, a question in his eyes, and a peach of a left hook already on its way. You can work out the speed he'd been moving at, and that's what I mean when I say that my Uncle James was quick and effective in everything he did.

So, appreciating this, and taking everything into account, my Uncle James turned back to the digging. He sighed a wee bit, for he felt very severely under-employed when he wasn't going a mile a minute, but for the sake of esprit de corps he slowed himself clean down to about the rate of a geriatric who's been sitting in a draught, and picked away at the trench. As a result of his leisurely pace he began to daydream.

Suddenly he heard a voice above him. 'Hey you'. He looked up. 'You there'. It was the foreman talking to him. 'Yes?' my Uncle James said. 'Is that the best you can do?' the foreman asked. 'Well', says my Uncle James, 'I can actually go quicker, but this is the speed I intend to finish at', and he turned to the old Welshman and the rest of his mates for agreement.

To his surprise they were all shovelling as if they were escaping prisoners of war. The whole squad was attacking the ground with their spades every bit as fast as my Uncle James had been when he first jumped down the trench. He looked up at the foreman, speechless. 'Well, I'll tell you one thing, Paddy', the foreman said, 'the speed you're going at's definitely the speed you're going to finish at. Because', he said, 'you're sacked'.

'And the moral of the story', my Uncle James used to tell us, 'is never trust a Welshman', but in all fairness I think he got the message wrong. My own idea of the moral is that you should always work at the speed you intend to finish at, but keep one eye open for the foreman while you're doing it.

On the Buses

In 1933, whenever I was only twelve, our Jack was a bus conductor with the Belfast Corporation. He ended up as an inspector with over forty years' service, but by the time he retired the city was hiving with inspectors; our Jack was far more important when he was a conductor. In those days it was bliss to have a job at all: to have a steady one was very heaven.

I had to take his lunch to the stop opposite to the New Lodge Road. Five full rounds of dip bread, with fried egg and bacon shoved into them, and the whole lot wrapped in the Belfast Telegraph till you could hardly bend the paper over. For some strange reason it was always tied up with wool.

Sometimes I would coax our Jack to give me a ride out to the terminus at Glengormley and back. All right, he would say, but sit there near the door and keep still.

I used to think it was brilliant. Whenever I climbed on board I used to look at our Jack's driver, Jack McWilliams, to see whether he would turn round and wink at me. If he did, I would flick my eyes at the downstairs passengers, to see if they'd noticed it.

It was the smell of the bus that I liked. Petrol. And the leather upholstery. And then the speed of it. When Jack McWilliams got out as far as Belfast

Castle at the foot of Ben Madigan, and not many people were getting on or off, he didn't half give that bus the works. Somehow I could never stop myself from getting up off my seat and standing on the platform, so that I could watch the road zipping away out of the tail of the bus. And then I would get a hold of the bar, so that I could look down at the shiny square setts from the very edge of the platform, but the next thing our Jack was nipping my arm as if he would have liked to take the skin off it. I thought I told you to sit there and keep still, he would say, you'll get me into trouble if you fall off this bus.

For the rest of the trip out I would sit and watch the way our Jack could write in his waybill, with his knees bent, taking the bumps like the under-carriage of an aeroplane.

Nowadays you wouldn't know the difference between Glengormley and any other part of the city, but in 1933 it was a country village, quiet and peaceful, with a couple of whitewashed cottages, and — a sure sign that you were outside the city — the distinct smell of cow manure. While our Jack and his driver got dug into their grub, I used to sit looking down their throats, hoping for a bit of soda bread and egg yolk.

At that time busmen knew their passengers so well that they would actually hold the bus for them at the stop, if they were late. And they would chat away to each other en route, the passengers complaining about their business problems, and the conductors sounding off about the inspectors. At Christmas time the passengers would leave wee parcels under the stairs, or slip the conductor a few bob. Our Jack used to land home with hundreds of cigarettes on Christmas

Eve. He had so many that he never even noticed the ones that our Jim and me used to knock off the minute his back was turned.

One odd thing that I learned at that time was that the conductor is in charge of the bus, in the same way that a captain is in charge of his ship — at all times. Our Jack learned it too, the hard way. They were belting along Stockman's Lane with an empty bus, heading for the depot; it was the first time our Jack or his driver had ever been that way. And what does Jack McWilliams do but try to drive under a bridge that was too low.

Their double-decker was converted instantly into a one-and-three-quarter-decker. Our Jack shot up the bottom deck like rice up a peashooter, ending up with bruises and contusions and murder in his heart for Jack McWilliams. But his troubles were far from over. 'You are both suspended for a fortnight,' the General Manager said. 'I can understand Blind Pew being suspended,' our Jack said to the boss, 'but why me?' 'Because,' said the General Manager, 'the conductor is in charge of the vehicle at all times.' 'Even when it's hitting bridges?' our Jack asked. 'Especially when it's hitting bridges,' the General Manager said.

There's one thing I must say, all the same. Our Jack certainly had the right temperament for working with the public. More so than our Billy. After the war he got our Billy a job conducting a trolley bus. It only lasted weeks. He went out to his work as if he was conducting a crusade to get the public off trolley buses altogether. Some poor unfortunate would offer him a pound note for a threepenny fare. 'I've no change,' our Billy would say, 'get off.' Bewildered and bemused, the poor individual would find himself on the street miles from home, and our Billy shaking his fist at him as he pulled the strap across the entrance. One day, after he threw a man off for offering him half a crown for a tuppenny fare at the start of his shift, some other man inside said loudly that he thought it was a shame. 'Oh, do you?' our Billy said, 'well in that case you can get off too.' 'What for?' the passenger asked. 'For annoying me,' our Billy said, giving the driver the emergency bell for the hundredth time that day.

He actually ended up hanging his bag and punch around the inspector's neck one day. That's how he resigned. It came as a relief to our Jack. It was an even bigger relief to the travelling public of Belfast.

The Morse Code Made Easy

During the war I went into Woolworth's in London North West Seven and bought a book called Teach Yourself Morse Code. I was supposed to pass an RAF exam. in it.

This book taught a very good system. For the Morse symbol in question it substituted a spoken phrase which had the same rhythm. For example the letter Y is dah dit dah dah, and this book taught the phrase: You Can Do Yours as a good way of remembering it. It's very good, isn't it?

Everywhere I went I was muttering to myself: You Can Do Yours, and other strange-sounding phrases like it. I got some very queer looks from people who happened to hear me, but I had it to learn and that was all about it.

Two Morse symbols that are very easy to mix up are Y and Q. Y is dah dit dah dah, and Q is dah dah dit dah. Very similar, aren't they? Well my wee book put an end to all confusion. Y was You Can Do Yours, but Q was God Save the Queen.

Now, if You Can Do Yours caused talk, you can guess what people thought when they heard me walking around saying God Save The Queen. It must have sounded like the opening lines of Hamlet, or something.

When the time came to take our test this officer sent Morse on a buzzer at four words a minute. It was the first time I had ever heard a buzzer.

It was money for jam. The thing was actually talking to me in the new language I had learned out of the book. Chase Me Charlie, it was saying, indicating to me that I was supposed to write down the letter C.

X Marks The Spot the buzzer said. I knew exactly what it meant. It meant the letter X — dah dit dit dah: down went X on my paper. I happened to notice the answer the fellow beside me wrote down. According to him L Marked the Spot.

After the test I must say I was dead confident. Sure enough the officer called out my name with the others who'd passed. Then he tested the successful ones, at six words a minute.

No bother. Freddie's Freezing, the buzzer announced — dit dit dah dit. Oh ho, says I, so Freddie's Freezing is he? Right. Down went the letter F. Dit dah dit dit — in London Town, says I, delighted with myself, putting L down.

Only one of us survived that, and that was me. I never enjoyed anything as much. 'It's a natural gift,' I told this Scotsman beside me, 'it indicates you've a brain like sheet lightning.'

'I'm going to send you eight words a minute now,' the officer told me, sitting on my own. Send away, says I, for I can understand your excitement. There's not many, says I, can sit down stone cold and knock off six words a minute, I'm certain sure.

Well eight words a minute wasn't easy. In fact, I found it very hard. I had no sooner sung God Save The Queen than I was into Chase Me Charlie and saying You Can Do Yours, right on top of it. I was burned out when the buzzing stopped.

'Well done,' the officer said, 'well done indeed.

Please wait behind.' They're probably going to make me into a Sergeant or something, I told myself. But here's what he actually said, when he got me on my own. 'We need picked people,' he said, 'for a special job, and you,' says he, 'fill the bill'.

Now back home my Uncle Alec had warned me about this. 'Steer clear,' he said, 'of special jobs and volunteer for nothing.' 'If you don't mind,' I said to this officer, 'I'm no good at special jobs.' but he put his arm on my shoulder and he says, 'My dear chap, you're a natural for what we have in mind. We need people who can operate a wireless transmitter, navigate the aircraft, and shoot the gun, that's what you are going to do.'

'Oh, is that a fact,' I said to him, 'well for your information I can't receive the Morse code at all. All I can do is say things like You Can Do Yours, and Chase me Charlie, that's all.'

'Well, whatever it is,' he said, 'it'll do the Royal Air Force.' He looked at me the way you look at a winning pools coupon. 'People like you are getting scarcer by the hour', he says. 'Why do you think that is?' I asked him. 'Because,' says he, 'they're being shot down like flies, that's why.'

'I wish to see the Commanding Officer,' I said.

'Laddie,' he says, 'go and pack your kitbag. You have an exciting time ahead of you. Your hours will be occupied in learning how to attack heavily defended harbours and convoys in daylight.'

'I want to see the Commanding Officer,' I repeated. 'Son', he said, 'you're looking at him.'

Shortly afterwards a window was flung open, and a copy of Teach Yourself Morse went fluttering down on to the busy London pavement. But it was too late.

By the time they'd finished with me in the Air Force I was doing twenty-four words a minute. That's one of the reasons why, if I don't watch myself, I still talk like a machine gun. Have you ever tried saying Chase Me Charlie at twenty-four words a minute?

The Battle of Britain

I'll not forget the Battle of Britain in a hurry, I'll tell you that much.

The first I knew of it some leading German was saying on the wireless that the game was up: there was no future for the Allied troops but working in the fields in Germany till we dropped.

That was in the middle of July, Nineteen and Forty. There was myself and three other RAF ground staff sitting in the canteen drinking beer. 'Oh ho,' says I, 'I don't fancy the sound of that too much. Working in the fields is it, eh?'

Wacker Davies looked at me with contempt: 'What are you worrying about,' he sneers, 'it'll probably be better than anything you've ever been used to in Ireland.'

That's when the Battle of Britain started for me. Wacker Davies was asking for it every bit as much as Hermann Goering and his Luftwaffe. The trouble was that this Liverpool man was able to give me about four stone, and he had that sort of indiarubber look that hard men nearly always have. I was going to have to box very clever, just like the Air Marshal in charge of the Spitfires. I swallowed that remark about Ireland and got on with the drinking.

It was looking very like an invasion, all right, coming into September that year. In fact they gave us a rifle each, and five rounds. That gave

Wacker Davies another chance to try out his wit. 'You and that rifle are so much alike,' he said, 'that I very nearly picked you up and sloped arms with you.' Then he busted out laughing, and gave me a playful dig' that nearly caved my ribs in. Take it easy, Sam, says I to myself: choose your ground before you give battle, I said. You don't get Air Chief Marshal Sir Hugh Dowding throwing all his fighters up at the one time for the Messerschmidts to snuff out, do you?

Coming into the middle of August the air battle was in full swing. Fighter stations and radar sites were being dive-bombed by JU88's and Stukas. This was Hitler's big push, all right. Over on the German farms they must have been getting the harness ready to strap the likes of me into the ploughs.

We were close enough to London to see bits of action — vapour trails, anti-aircraft fire, and even the odd German aeroplane. One of them flew right over our aerodrome one day: 'I suppose it comes from France,' I said to Jake Thompson, a Scotch mate of mine. The next thing I knew somebody was imitating me: 'I suppose it comes from France,' in a terrible attempt at the Belfast accent. I looked round and got a jet of hundred octane petrol right up the gub. Wacker Davies had been filling up one of the aircraft, and he had turned the hose on me. He was roaring with laughter: 'That'll clean you up a bit,' he shouts, 'it's a good while since you had a bath.'

Waiting for the petrol to dry off I told myself that the battle was reaching a critical phase. I'm just like one of these fighter pilots, I said, I'll have to wait for the exact moment before I can shout Tally Ho.

The moment came at the end of September — a very important date in the Battle of Britain. Down at the flight one day, when the aircraft were up and we were all killing time, Wacker tramped on my corn. On purpose, at that. Before I could stop myself I had belted him one on the whiskers. 'Right, that does it,' he says, 'you and me's gonna fight.'

Well, you know what Englishmen are like — they immediately began to organise things. 'Form a ring,' they all shouted, 'form a ring, there. Paddy and Wacker are going to have a fight,' they said. 'Fight fair, now,' somebody said, and somebody else mentioned a stop watch, for two-minute rounds.

This didn't suit me, of course. I decided to put myself into the position known to fighter pilots as 'up sun.' 'Take that coat off, before I beat it off you,' I said to Wacker. He started to peel it off, eagerly. I waited till his arms were nicely caught up in the sleeves, and then I lifted a wooden chock off the ground, and nearly cleaved the head off him with it.

Never before, in the field of human conflict, did anybody get such a surprise. He hit the deck like a tigerskin rug. Before he knew what had happened, his mates were slapping his cheeks and telling him that his name was Wacker Davies. Whenever he came round later on he was buying me pints, and claiming that his parents had Irish blood in them.

Funny enough, as it turned out, Winston Churchill won his particular battle that day too.

But I'll tell you one thing — he didn't do as clean a job of it as I did.

Carbuncles

There used to be a man came round our street in Tiger's Bay called Mister Robinson. His name was actually Norman Robinson but nobody in Cosgrave Street would have dreamt of using his Christian name. He was the man who fixed people up with drapery on tick. He dressed our whole family for years, Mister Robinson. He was also the man who first introduced me to bunions and carbuncles.

He was in his middle fifties then, meaning he'd be over a hundred if he's still living. A nice man, Mister Robinson, low set and plump: always sweating with the steep walk up our street, and always, always complaining about his feet and legs. 'It's the bunions, Missus', he would gasp to Mother, taking a chair and stretching his feet out in front of him. Each of his shoes was slit twice just by the big toe, giving it as much room to expand as a camel would nearly need.

'And then over and above the bunions I'm open to the carbuncles', Mister Robinson would add. Mother would be going tsk tsk tsk, but I would be sitting staring at his feet, riveted.

Carbuncles and bunions. What on earth were they? I imagined a carbuncle as being something like those cockle things that I had seen on horses' legs. I pictured Mister Robinson's legs covered with them.

But bunions? I must admit they had me beaten. Were they extra toes grown at right angles? Were they like onions? I couldn't contain my curiosity. I asked Mister Robinson what exactly were carbuncles and bunions. 'D'ye mind?' he said to Mother. She didn't, so he took both socks off. To my deep disappointment bunions were just bumps on the south side of the big toe. 'What about the carbuncles?' I said eagerly, but there was no way that Mister Robinson was going either to roll his trousers up or slide them down to show me. He just patted the backs of both legs. 'I'm very much open to carbuncles', he said. 'I must be run down'. So in the absence of visual proof I thought for years as I say that carbuncles were like those cockle things on horses' legs. Until I got them myself, that is, in 1943, in the Western Desert: one on the back of each leg.

Merciful heavens let me never forget it. Talk about your carbuncles! These daisies would have won prizes. As I was lying in bed, excused duty, I thought often about that poor tick man in Cosgrave Street. It's no wonder says I you complained so much. Bunions is one thing, but God take care of us bunions and carbuncles at the same time — you deserved the Victoria Cross, Mister Robinson, and I'm saying it now when I should have told you to your face.

A year later I found myself near Athens trying to puzzle out why I was all of a sudden fighting Greeks when I had enlisted to fight Germans, when what do you think happened? You've guessed it. The carbuncles came back. Two beauties, one on each leg.

They did what the ouzo and the retsina wine had never managed to do — they put me clean off my feet. I ended up in the military hospital.

I was only in there for four days. On the morning of the third day I was held down screaming and swearing by an army of nursing auxiliaries whilst my carbuncles were fixed up. But it was on the afternoon of that day that General Alexander visited the hospital, you know the one who became a Field Marshal.

All the patients were lined up in the corridor outside their own rooms, when along came the General. I could hear snatches of his conversation with the other patients, who were all soldiers.

'Ah, the arm I see', the general said to somebody whose arm was in a sling. 'Where did it happen?' 'Anzio', the man told him. 'Jolly bad luck', the general said, as he moved up.

'Ah, a facial wound'. This time he was addressing an Egyptian mummy. 'Where did you get it?' 'Salerno', the mummy told him. 'Jolly bad luck', General Alexander said, then he stopped in front of me.

I was wearing shorts. The bandages on my legs could be clearly seen. 'Ah', said the general, 'the legs, I see'. I said yes: yes it was the legs all right. 'Where did it happen?' General Alexander asked. 'Mersa Matruh', I said, knowing rightly it was going to lead to complications. The general blinked. There had been no fighting in Mersa Matruh for two years. 'Taking a long time to clear up, isn't it?' he asked. 'Carbuncles', I told him, seriously, 'are very hard to clear up'. General Alexander looked at me, puzzled. He obviously didn't know what carbuncles were. I suddenly had the most overpowering temptation to tell him that carbuncles were those wee cockle things that you see on horses' legs, but just in time the colonel in charge of the hospital whispered something in the great man's ear. 'Jolly bad luck', the general said to me, and moved, with some relief I thought, towards a Scottish captain who had been bombed by the American Air Force.

Officer Material

Whenever I was out abroad during the war I became very friendly with an American millionaire. Well at least everybody said he was a millionaire. This fellow was a pilot on our squadron. His name was Chris, and his surname appears to this day on all sorts of electrical appliances.

He was a very nice fellow this Chris. He was a Warrant Officer in the Air Force, which is to say he couldn't go any higher unless he became a commissioned officer.

And that is just what he couldn't be. For millionaire or no millionaire, up till then the Royal Air Force had never invited your man to appear in front of one of their commissioning boards. He used to talk about it to me in the tent. About the fact that his brother was an RAF officer and he wasn't. It annoyed him a bit.

I say he used to talk to me about it, but actually I was an expert in those days at letting on to listen to people and going ahead with my own thoughts. While Chris was puzzling out his problem in a pained sort of a way I used to be sitting looking at him, the picture of polite attention. But all the time I was asking myself why I wasn't sitting in the Gibraltar Bar in York Street in Belfast murdering pints of porter and making a fortune off the novice chasers, instead of sitting in Tripoli surrounded by Bedouins and Senussi and flies and beetles and things.

'What do you want to be an officer for?' I used to ask Chris, whenever he did get through. 'Aren't you a millionaire for goodness sake?'

Of course he never answered that direct. I wouldn't think many millionaires are actually used to being spoken to like that, but he would deal with the first half of it. 'Other people are made officers,' he would drawl. 'I should be one as well. Do you think it's because the Commanding Officer's an Irishman?'

'The trouble with you', I said, 'is that you're too law abiding. You're too quiet. Terry Ward from Galway', says I, 'used to run up one side of the Commanding Officer's tent in the middle of the night when he got drunk, and slide down the other side shouting, "Come out and fight for your country!" and they made him an officer. That,' I said, 'is how they expect an officer to behave'. 'Do you think so?' he asked me. Then he sat for a good while thinking it over, but he finally shook his head. He couldn't do that sort of thing, Chris. He was too well brought up. Millionaires are all like that.

Well what do you think happened but one day didn't the Commanding Officer call me over. 'What's that you've got on, Sergeant?' he asked me, meaning the German hat and the jackboots that I used to run about in. 'It's a German hat and jackboots', I told him. 'Well', he says, 'dig your proper uniform out for you're in front of the commissioning board soon'.

I don't know how I ever got round to telling Chris. And when I did his mouth fell open. "No wonder your mouth's falling open', says I, 'sure I did the same myself when the CO told me.

'D'you think' says I, 'they've got their records mixed up?'

'My God', says your man Chris, 'you've shaved all the hair off your head and you run about in a German hat and jackboots. Not only that', he goes on, 'but every time you go to Alexandria on leave there's a string of complaints from the military police. What kind of a system does the Air Force use?'

'Don't worry about it', I told him, 'there's one sure thing that's going to wreck me on this board'. 'What's that?' says he. 'It's what my father does', I said. 'They always ask you what your father does'. 'Well', says Chris, 'and what does your father do?' 'He's a donkeyman', says I, 'on the boats'. Chris looked doubtful. 'Seriously, Paddy', he said, 'I sure hope you get it, but. . . . .donkeyman', he shook his head. 'I just can't see it'.

Sure enough up came the catch question. 'We must ask you', said this Group Captain apologetically, 'what line is your father in'? 'Actually', I said, 'he's in the Head Line. He's a donkeyman', says I.

The four senior officers leaned forward interestedly. 'A donkeyman?' they said, 'what's that?' So I enjoyed myself giving them all the facts about the stokehold and the engine room. 'How jolly interesting', they all said. 'And what are your plans for post-war?' the president asked me next. 'Do you know what my ambition is?' I said. They shook their heads. 'I would love', says I, 'to be a tramp: tramping all over Ireland, eating bread and cheese, and people buying me pints'. They were all ears. 'Right enough', says one of them. 'I think many of us should re-adjust our criteria'. Since I didn't know what he was talking about I nodded and said it didn't sound like a bad idea at all.

When I went back and told Chris he said 'Tough luck, Paddy. I guess you and I are going to be together for some time to come'. 'I would be inclined to think so', I said, but then came surprise number two. 'You're moving into the Officers' Mess', the Commanding Officer told me about three weeks later, 'so stop acting the goat in that German hat and jackboots'.

Chris shook hands with me, when I had to move out of the tent.

'D'you know what you want to do', I told him. 'What', he says. 'You want to put about that your old man's lost all his money at the horses', says I, 'then shave your head, start wearing that German hat and jackboots and hit the first man you meet a belt on the gob. If you're not made an officer after that', says I, 'well then my old man's a millionaire donkeyman'.

The Pathfinder

At the end of a street of Georgian houses near Queen's University one house is sealed, tight as a tomb. In the evenings, outside this house, a tiny group of winos gather.

Their ages range from thirty to sixty. Their faces are grey and their wits are slow. They don't bother the students who live in the area very much. Advanced alkies are gentle people: these ones cadge, but timidly, and only for pence. They sit together on the steps of the doorless house, and share a bottle, and murmur in low voices, like old arabs round the hookah. Then, round about midnight, they drift away, no trouble to anybody at all.

But one winter's night the winos left someone behind on the top step, leaning against the wall, eyes shut, head to the side, as if he was listening.

Taffy was his name. The cops knew him as harmless: just too fond of the electric soup. He was quiet, and liked to go his own way, so the others left him, after tugging gently at his sleeve. The winos went away into the darkness, hanging together for company, and Taffy went out of their minds for good.

A cop found him at five in the morning, still sitting there. His head had fallen forward, and his hands hung limply down, in the classic drunken pose. The cop called an ambulance on the RT, and, since there was just the faintest trace of a sparrow's heartbeat in him it was the hospital he went to, and not the morgue.

Taffy went into intensive care. They took off his clothes and sponged him, and put a white gown on him: the gown fastened up the front, and showed his long sticks of legs and his drowned skin. The doctor gave him oxygen. His body temperature went up soon after, but not very much, even though it was so warm in intensive care that the nurses wore hardly anything under their thin dresses.

Both the doctor and the staff nurse shook their heads when they put the stethoscope to him. His lungs were awash. Taffy lay, quite still, long and lean in the bed, filling the whole length of it, and only half its width. His eyelids seemed almost transparent. The nurse entered dots on a graph. She looked at him, and gave a resigned nod. This wasn't the first Taffy she'd seen. She went to catch up on some paper work.

Outside, in Reception, the clerk was putting Taffy's possessions into an envelope. Eight pence, and an RAF discharge. And also a bronze set of wings, about three inches long. The money and the discharge book had been in his pocket, but the wings had been pinned to his dirty, greasy serge jacket, on the left hand side, like a row of medals.

The clerk had filled envelopes for bigger nutters than Taffy in his time. He just shrugged, dropped the wings in, and sealed the flap.

Back in the ward, the day cleaning woman plugged her machine into the wall socket. The staff nurse, passing by Taffy's bed, suddenly stopped, and looked at the quiet figure: then she carried on, frowning. She could have sworn she had heard him say something. But it was impossible. Not in his state.

The day cleaner pressed the button and the electric motor hummed. She began to polish an already gleaming floor.

Both the nurse and the day cleaner would have been astonished to learn that Taffy could hear the motor: that, in fact, he had been listening for it.

It had started on his orders. 'Contact,' he had said firmly, and the port outer engine had exploded into life. In seconds the other three were spitting and snarling too. Taffy returned the ground sergeant's thumbs-up sign, and the bomber squealed and groaned its way to the runway mouth. He switched on his microphone. 'We're in business,' he told his crew. 'You bet,' they replied, 'good old Taffy!'

'You are clear to take off,' the tower told him, and the caravan gave him a green lamp. The engineer moved the throttles forward and the black Lancaster flung itself between the rows of white markers, over the perimeter track, and up into the circuit. The wheels thumped into their housings, the bomber edged on to a climbing course that would take it to the enemy coast, and Taffy relaxed, and touched his Pathfinder's badge for luck.

The bronze wings were his lucky charm. The other crew members had their rabbits' paws, and girls' scarves and so on, but for Taffy the Pathfinder's wings were enough. The proudest day of his life had been the day he pinned them on his left tunic pocket.

The Lancaster was running sweetly, on course, at operational height. Taffy turned his eyes to the eastern sky, and smiled. . .

. . . .Leaning over him, the staff nurse turned his head to the side, and gently closed the gaping mouth. Then she drew the sheet up until it covered his long, white hair.

This one, she thought, had departed exactly on target.

Thoughts on the Silicon Chip

Everybody seems to be steamed up about the silicon chip these days. The Irish Congress of Trade Unions is keeping a wary eye on it, in case it does the work of too many people, and the top management men are watching it in the hope that that's exactly what it will do. Some magazine's calling its discovery the last frontier of science, but you can more or less ignore that — I've known a time when the zip fastener got the same sort of rave notices.

My own advice is to wait and see. There was a great period of euphoria when the electric bacon slicer reached the shop counter but a good many grocers' thumbs were cut off before a proper appreciation of the machine's potential was arrived at.

All these things are relative. Take television: as far as I was concerned it was only a gimmick right up to the late 1950's. I saw a TV show over in London round about the 1955 mark, and I found it hard to believe that John Logie Baird's family would want to be associated with the invention. It was easily the worst form of entertainment I had ever seen, bar the British musical film. Everybody seemed to wear evening dress and speak in choked Oxford accents: 'I think I'll stick to the wireless,' says I, 'at least that way we don't have to look at them.'

But a couple of years later what happens? I'm flying at the horses: no matter what I touch turns to gold: other punters are rubbing up against me for luck: I'm touching for doubles and trebles all over the place, and I've even bought myself a new suit, when somebody tells me that you can see the English racing on the TV in Mickey Hamill's bar on the Falls Road. 'So what,' says I, 'sure you can see it in the pictures.' 'Ah,' this fellow says, 'but in Mickey Hamill's you can see it as it's actually happening.'

Well, that put a totally different complexion on things, of course. To watch racing actually taking place? I'd never been to a racecourse in my life. Indeed, the only man I'd ever met who had been to a racecourse was our Jim: he'd been to the Maze racing to do clerking for a small-time bookie one time. They ended up skinned. The bookie was so windy that he refused to lay favourites, and unfortunately five out of the six races were won by second favourites. Our Jim had to lend this bookie his train fare home: he never saw the money again. But one thing our Jim did tell me was that the only way to make money at the horses was to go to the course. 'You can easily see the horses that are not meant to win,' he explained, 'the jockeys nearly pull the heads off them going up to the post.' I got a trolleybus smartly to Mickey Hamill's.

Now before I go any further I have to tell you that I was carrying money to the extent of three figures at this time. I was on the crest of a wave. My minimum stake was a fiver. I was beginning to make a name for myself in downtown Belfast as a debonair punter known to have the length of a score of quid on a horse.

Well, it was quite true that the racing was live on the TV. It was before the days of Ulster Television, so it was the English signal we were having to watch. The reception was terrible, the horses were only blurs and wriggles, but the sound commentary could be heard clearly enough, so I began to punt.

Merciful sweet heavens, let me not think on it. What a lambasting I got that day. There were four races on the box; only one of them was worth the risking of the money, the other three were races that I would normally have left severely alone; the horses in them were only a jump ahead of the boneyard. But this is the fatal flaw in TV racing to this very day — just because it's live, the punter is enticed on to races that are about as easy to read as a woman's mind.

To cut a long story short, I was wiped out. I walked into Mickey Hamill's bar a self-confident, dynamic, purposeful, rich man: I tottered out a wreck, afraid to look the world in the eye, with not even the price of a pint on me.

So much for television: they say it brought the world into our living rooms. Well, all it did for me was to ruin my prospects: if I hadn't been enticed to watch the screen that day I might have owned my own bookie's business by now. It wasn't much of a scientific breakthrough for me.

These things are relative. Definitely. The silicon chip's only an extension of the zip fastener. In fact, I can extend it even further back. Fifty years ago there was a woman in Cosgrave Street, where I was brought up, and her husband used to keep her very short of money. On top of that she hadn't even a chair in the house: her man broke them all over her back, and then put them on the fire.

Well one day she happened to find a shilling in the street. She couldn't believe her great good fortune. She planked the shilling over the weekend till she worked out her options. Finally she made up her mind: she went down York Street to a second hand shop, and she bought a mangle.

The mangle was delivered to the backyard, and this woman just sat looking at it, and crying with happiness. The mangle was her silicon chip.

Her man came home that night, and she said nothing — just waited for him to see it. Eventually he got up to go to the yard, opened the door and stopped stone dead. 'What d'ye call that?' he said. She smiled with simple pride: 'It's a mangle,' she said, 'it'll be a great help: my poor hands are destroyed, wringing your long drawers out.'

He turned round, grabbed a hold of her, and hit her a looter across the side of the jaw. 'What's that for?' she wanted to know.

'I can stand many a thing in a woman,' he said, 'but one thing I'm not going to tolerate in this house is bone laziness.'

The Semi-D

Andy was at the lorry driving for a timber concern, but the owner went bust. Then he wrought in the aircraft factory as a riveter, but he couldn't get any more than the flat forty hour week out of it, so that was no good. He tried working as a barman, and then he went on the knocker selling encyclopaedia, but all the time the semi-d. that he had set his heart on for his dark-haired Christine was fading further away in the distance.

Then they both noticed the television adverts belting away there for prison officers. The money was great, there was a mortgage allowance and you named your own overtime, so Andy had a crack at it.

Once the training was over and he was given a uniform and a proper shift routine at the jail, they got their first jolt:

'The woman in the flat upstairs is worried about her husband,' Christine told Andy. 'Oh,' says he, 'and why would that be?'

'She doesn't want the gunmen to mistake him for you,' Christine said, 'and she thinks we should leave.'

'Tell her we'll not be here to worry her that much longer,' he told her, 'the semi-d.'s only a matter of weeks away now.' But they both fell silent when he said it.

The ready money was certainly piling up, but

for the job itself, it wasn't long before Andy got a sickener. He was on supervision duty once, during the visiting period, and a wee boy of about four broke away from his parents. Andy hunkered down and spread his arms, and made a face for a bit of fun, for his attachment for kids was all the stronger on account of Christine not being able to have any. But the prisoner grabbed the youngster up and turned him away from Andy: 'Keep your hands off my child, you bastard ye,' the prisoner said. He was in for a doorstep killing, this fellow.

Later Christine told Helen, a friend of hers, about it: 'Andy was awful upset so he was,' she said, 'sure there was no need to bring a wee child into it.'

The day came when they moved into their semi-d., and they filled it full of lovely furnishings and wall-to-wall carpet, and an illuminated fish tank. But Andy was paying a heavy price for it. He truly detested every hour of the work, and he had long, long hours to put in. Yet, if they were to keep their semi-d. then he couldn't leave the job.

In a way, he was just as much a prisoner there as the bombers and gunmen he was guarding. In fact, it put him on the bottle. He even got into the habit of nipping into a pub across the road from the jail at lunch time — Andy, who never would have thanked you for a drink through the day.

And that's how they killed him.

He'd been too regular at it. They were waiting in a van outside the pub.

He was easy meat, coming out exactly on time.

Of course there was a whole noration. All sorts of notables called at the house, and the neighbours in the other semi-d.'s peeped out through their curtains at the bishop, and the politicians, and the police with the scrambled egg on their caps. 'Don't you worry about your mortgage,' some councillor said to Christine, 'the Government'll look after all that for you.' But Christine didn't know what he was talking about. She was under sedation. Funny enough, all she could think about was what she would make Andy for his supper. For all his slim build he was right and fond of the grub. Maybe a bit of roast ham, he liked the roast ham, with pickles.

The funeral was something fierce. Andy's workmates carried the coffin, and cameramen ran backwards ahead of it. The minister's funeral address made all the papers the next day, and as well as that some politician said that security was a disgrace. Christine's head was singing all through the service, and she kept looking down at her feet, so that she wouldn't have to see the coffin, with the black uniform hat on top of it. It had never suited him. No uniform would ever have suited Andy.

Afterwards Christine tried stopping with her mother, but in a couple of weeks a terrible fidgeting came over her. 'I want to go back to the semi-d.' she said, and so she did, by herself.

Helen, her friend, tried to get Christine interested in dressmaking, or baking, or even just having her over to visit, but no, she said, no, she didn't want to go out.

Naturally, Christine's mother worried about it. 'She only wants to be on her own,' she told Helen, 'just cleaning and fussing round that house all the time. I've asked her to sell it and come in with me, not to stay so much on her own. But she won't. She says she'll never in a million years sell that semi-d.'

Helen nodded: 'I know,' she said, 'sure I came past it on the way up here. Christine was that busy out at the front that she never even saw me. She was actually cleaning the gate: imagine cleaning the gate. Do you know this? She even leaned over and put her cheek on it: just touched it like.'

Christine's mother shook her head and drew her lips in: 'It's desperate altogether,' she sighed, 'just desperate.'